You can't <u>say</u> that to me!

Other Books by Suzette Haden Elgin

NONFICTION

Genderspeak: Men, Women, and the Gentle Art of Verbal Self-Defense
The Gentle Art of Verbal Self-Defense
More on the Gentle Art of Verbal Self-Defense
The Last Word on the Gentle Art of Verbal Self-Defense
Success with the Gentle Art of Verbal Self-Defense
Staying Well with the Gentle Art of Verbal Self-Defense
The Gentle Art of Written Self-Defense

TEXTBOOKS

Guide to Transformational Grammar
(with John Grinder, Ph.D.)
Pouring Down Words
What Is Linguistics?

NOVELS

The Communipaths
Furthest
At the Seventh Level
Twelve Fair Kingdoms
The Grand Jubilee
And Then There'll Be Fireworks
Star-Anchored, Star-Angered
Native Tongue
Yonder Comes the Other End of Time
Native Tongue II: The Judas Rose
Native Tongue III: Earthsong

Audio Programs by Suzette Haden Elgin

Mastering the Gentle Art of Verbal Self-Defense
Success with the Gentle Art of Verbal Self-Defense
The Gentle Art of Verbal Self-Defense for Parents and Kids
(with Rebecca Haden, M.A.)
The Gentle Art of Verbal Self-Defense for Parents and Teenagers
(with Rebecca Haden, M.A.)

You can't say that to me!

Stopping the Pain
of Verbal Abuse—
An 8-Step Program

Suzette Haden Elgin, Ph.D.

John Wiley & Sons, Inc.

Copyright © 1995 by Suzette Haden Elgin
All rights reserved. Published simultaneously in Canada.

This publication is designed to provide accurate and authoritative information in regard to the subject matter covered. It is sold with the understanding that the publisher is not engaged in rendering professional services. If legal, accounting, medical, psychological, or any other expert assistance is required, the services of a competent professional person should be sought.

Library of Congress Cataloging-in-Publication Data:

Elgin, Suzette Haden.
    You can't say that to me! : stopping the pain of verbal abuse : an 8-step program / Suzette Haden Elgin.
        p. cm.
    Includes bibliographical references and index.
    ISBN 0-471-00395-6 (alk. paper). — ISBN 0-471-00399-9 (pbk. : alk. paper)
        1. Verbal self-defense.   2. Invective.   3. Threat (Psychology)
I. Title.
BF637.V47E4337   1994
153.6 — dc20   94-36128

Printed in the United States of America

20 19 18 17 16 15 14 13 12 11

Preface

Everyone whose life includes verbal abuse has to come to some
sort of conclusion about the *source* of all that poisonous language.
We know it doesn't fall from the sky like rain; but it seems almost
as mysterious — and as much beyond our control — as the weather
does. We tend to feel that verbal abuse is the product of human
wickedness and human weakness. We tend to assume that verbal
abusers do what they do because they are evil, and because they
either enjoy causing pain or are willing to hurt others as long as it
furthers their own selfish goals. We tend to assume that verbal
victims are helpless in the face of this overwhelming force and
that their only hope for anything better is to find *good* people to
spend their time with. If that option is closed to them (perhaps
because their abuser is their boss or their spouse or their parent or
their child) we feel that they must simply learn to live with their
problem.

This book will show you that these feelings are based on misconceptions and traditional errors. It will demonstrate to you that
you can, in fact, have a life in which verbal abuse almost never
happens and in which — on those rare occasions when it can't be
avoided — you are able to deal with it expertly and without the
usual negative consequences. This is a benefit valuable beyond
measure — because verbal abuse is literally dangerous to your
health and safety and well-being. Nothing you can do is more
likely to change your life dramatically for the better than getting
rid of verbal abuse in your own language environment.

The Eight Steps

In Steps 1 and 2, you will learn that both the problem of verbal abuse and the problem's solution have their sources not in the people who are communicating so badly, not in their characters or their personalities, but in language itself. And you will learn what people get *from* verbal abuse that makes them willing to tolerate its negative effects.

Step 3 explains that, far from being helpless, far from having no option but to hope for a miracle, you already *have* everything you need to solve the problem of verbal violence in your life. Whether you are a verbal abuser or a verbal victim (or both), this book speaks to your needs, demonstrating to you that you are already equipped to solve this problem for yourself. You don't need to take a course or hire an expert or buy some fancy gadget. You need only your own skill as a speaker of your language and your reliable common sense. This section also explains where the confusion about verbal abuse came from and how the misunderstandings have come to be so pervasive.

Because most people in our society have accepted the myth that expert language skills are only for the very lucky and the elite, Step 4 focuses on proving to you that you are an expert in your own language, and that your personal knowledge base about your language is far superior to anything you could find in a textbook.

In Step 5 the focus is on learning how to recognize and defuse hostile language, and on why it's critically important to do so. Not only because verbal abuse leads to illness but because it also leads to injury — because it is where *physical* violence begins.

Step 6 takes up the question of how — when you've decided not to take part in verbal abuse any more — you can follow *through* on that decision in spite of the barriers of competitiveness and guilt. Step 7 explains how and why the language of one person has the power to bring about change in the language of others: This phenomenon makes the situation of the victim of verbal abuse very different from that of other victims. Finally, Step 8 offers a careful discussion of the need to take responsibility for your own language and the means you have available to you for doing so.

How the Eight Steps Are Structured

Each chapter presents one of the eight steps and has the following structure:

- A scenario that shows ordinary people involved in abusive language interactions: husband and wife, parent and child, doctor and patient, teacher and student, mother and daughter-in-law, employer and employee.

- An analysis of the scenario that makes the basis for the conflict clear. And because the people involved in verbal confrontations rarely agree on what they are really about, the analysis includes the personal viewpoint of each of the characters in the scenario.

- One or more language techniques specifically designed to deal with the conflict shown in the scenario.

- A return to the scenario, to show how use of the technique just introduced would have changed it for the better.

- A set of backup exercises and activities, plus carefully chosen quotations — Sight Bites — from various sources, to help you put all of this information to use in your own life.

Acknowledgments

This book is the eighth in a series of books on a communication system called *The Gentle Art of Verbal Self-Defense.* It's also the *Gentle Art* book I would have written *first* in that series, if I had known how — I didn't. It took the more than twenty years I've spent working with the system, and the help of thousands of people who were willing to work *with* me, to teach me what I really needed to know before I started. It pleases me greatly to find myself able to write this book at last, and I am grateful to John Wiley & Sons for supporting me so generously and so enthusiastically in the effort.

I can't list the thousands of people I've just mentioned, though I owe each one several lines of thanks. I especially wish I could thank every single person who has written me to say, "I just finished reading your book, and it helped; I only wish I'd read it years ago." You know who you are; thank you for writing. My grateful thanks to all of you who have worked with me as my students, as my clients, as my trainers, and in my seminars; you have been my constant and always reliable source of data about communication in the real world. My thanks to *all* my readers; not only those who read the books but also the readers of my newsletters, which could not be written without the constant flow of materials you send me and the answers you write to my endless questions. I am grateful to all my past editors, and especially to the copy editors who've had the thankless task of fixing my errors, struggling with my native Ozark English dialect, and unscrambling my word-tangles.

On the list of people whose names I *must* mention here: My

graduate adviser at the University of California San Diego, linguist Leonard Newmark, who taught me everything I know about how to make people want to learn and how to convince them to come eagerly to the learning experience. Linguist John Grinder, who helped me at the very beginning of my work with the *Gentle Art* system, especially when I had to fight my way through thickets of scientific jargon and gibberish. Navajo linguist and educator Kathy Begaye Tom, who taught me how *English* works by letting me study it through the lens of Navajo. Dr. Virginia Satir, whose brilliant insights and methods in family therapy have been invaluable to me over the years. My daughter (and colleague) Rebecca Haden Chomphosy, who has always been ready with her encouragement and her usefully different way of perceiving this world; she has often made it possible for me to step outside the frame I would otherwise have been trapped in so that I could see and hear and feel with more clarity and more skill. My long-suffering husband, George, and all our children and grandchildren, who have provided me with the best of my examples and dialogues, together with the opportunity to hone my verbal self-defense skills daily. My editor at John Wiley & Sons, PJ Dempsey, who has contributed greatly to making this book possible and has been patient with me far beyond the call of duty. Thank you, one and all.

My work would have been impossible without that of many others ahead of me whose wisdom I could call on. I have tried hard to credit every one of these individuals since Cicero and Aristotle, to cite them in my notes and list them in my bibliography; if I have missed anyone, it is by chance and not by intention. I am especially indebted to the work of Paul Watzlawick, Gregory Bateson, Edward T. Hall, George Miller, Noam Chomsky, Ronald Langacker, Cheris Kramarae, and Sally McConnell-Ginet.

If you have comments about this book, or questions to ask, I would always be pleased to hear from you; feel free to write to me directly, any time.

Suzette Haden Elgin, Ph.D.
P.O. Box 1137
Huntsville, Arkansas 72740-1137

Contents

How to Use This Book

There are two ways to use this book. One is simply to read all of its chapters, as you would read any other book, without giving your attention to the Backup sections that conclude each chapter. This will provide you with a broad base of information about verbal abuse, verbal abusers and their victims, and verbal self-defense. Knowing the facts and becoming aware of the myths will always help. Understanding that there *are* specific actions you can take to end verbal abuse, even if you don't decide to move in that direction yourself, will always improve matters. A great deal of the misery caused by verbal abuse is due to nothing more than a lack of information, and reading this book will go a long way toward repairing that information shortfall.

The other way to use the book is to supplement your reading by working through the Backup sections (an "Index to Backup Material" precedes the main index). This will not only give you the advantages just described, but will also provide you with practice in putting the information to *use*. The backups will help you do all of the following:

- Become aware of the patterns of verbal abuse in your life: when and where it occurs; who is most often the abuser or the victim; what strategies you tend to use in hostile interactions; the results you get from those strategies; what effects abusive language has on you and on those around you.

- Become aware of the myths about language and language behavior that you have relied on in the past, and that have kept you from realizing that you do *not* have to suffer the consequences of verbal abuse.

- Become *consciously* aware of much information that has always been yours, but that has been well below the level of your conscious awareness, so that you are able to make systematic deliberate use of your knowledge.

- Try out the verbal self-defense techniques presented in the book, in privacy, at your own speed and at your own convenience — both for hypothetical situations and for language interactions in your own life.

- Observe the changes that occur in your life as you begin actively using the information and the verbal self-defense techniques, so that you can track your progress.

To take advantage of this feature, you need only an ordinary three-ring binder and a supply of notebook paper (or, if you are someone who genuinely dislikes writing, a tape recorder and a supply of blank tapes). The Backup sections give you careful instructions and will lead you step by step through a wide variety of exercises and activities; all you have to do is follow the simple directions.

The Benefits You Can Expect

You can expect to gain a substantial and significant improvement in your own health and well-being. It's not possible to be healthy and stay fit in an environment of constant hostility and stress. The human body and mind are not designed to remain perpetually poised and ready for combat and crisis and struggle. Eliminating verbal abuse from your life will do more to make you truly *well* than any amount of money and time you might spend for medical procedures and products or in health clubs and spas.

You can expect to be able to do *more, and to do it far better, in both your personal and your professional life.* When your energies aren't constantly being drained by the need to deal with conflict, your productivity and creativity increase automatically. It's not that *you* have changed, but that you can turn all of your resources to positive efforts instead of wasting them in endless arguments and the dreary process of recovering from arguments. Verbal abuse is exhausting for the abuser, the victim, and the involved bystanders who are, indirectly, also victims. *It wears you out.*

You can expect a dramatic change for the better in your relationships with other people. Perhaps you have been someone whose company everyone avoids. Perhaps every interaction you have with others seems to turn out badly. Perhaps your home has been more like a war zone than a refuge and a place of comfort, because nobody can talk about any subject there without fighting about it. Perhaps you have had to go to work every day knowing that you would spend much of your time being chewed out, belittled, and tormented by your boss or by a colleague. Perhaps you have been a boss who knows that he or she is cordially detested by employees and knows no way to turn that around. You don't have to go on living in these negative environments; you can change them. These are problems you can fix.

The benefits of your efforts aren't restricted to you personally. When you put this program into practice, you are doing something — something truly effective — to reduce the level of violence in our society. Violence is our *worst* problem; if we could get it under even moderate control, we would have the resources necessary to tackle all our other problems. You may have thought that because you are just one person there's nothing you can do — that's false. Violence doesn't begin on the streets or in the media; it begins in our homes. When the only model children and young people see for handling conflict is verbal combat, that is the only strategy they learn. They go on to be adults who know no other way to resolve a disagreement except to *fight* about it — and who then can provide only that model for *their* children. This endless vicious cycle is more responsible for the current epidemic of crime and brutality in the United States than any other factor; and unlike the media, it's something over which you actually have a great deal of control. When you work through this eight-step program you are taking action to *end* that cycle. For once, you can do something for *yourself* that at the same time does something for others, both for those near and dear to you and for society as a whole.

Yes, you DO understand.

Yes, you ARE a language expert.

Yes, you CAN communicate successfully and end verbal abuse in your life.

Let's begin.

Introduction

"Will you PLEASE explain WHY you can't do ANYthing RIGHT?"

"WHAT'S THE MATTER with you, ANYway? Have you LOST your MIND?"

"Your BEHAVIOR is disGUSTing, and I am NOT going to put UP with it any longer!"

"I suppose you think you're SMART, DON'T you? YOU think you did pretty WELL! RIGHT? Well, let me tell YOU . . . "

"And just WHAT does that LOOK on your face MEAN, I'd like to know?? Can't you take a JOKE, FOR CRYING OUT LOUD?"

"I'm sure you thought you would be able to do this, dear, and it's not your fault that you're having a hard time. We all understand why it's too much for you, dear."

Does this all sound familiar? Is it the story of your life?

"Hey, I was just KIDDing! What's your PROBlem, are you PARANOID?"

"YOU can't follow even the SIMPlest inSTRUCtions, CAN you? How'd you GET this job, ANyway — win it in a LOTTERY?"

"GOODness! THAT outfit almost makes you look THIN!"

"If you REALLY cared about your family, YOU'D get a decent JOB!"

1

"Mommies that LOVE their little girls aren't MEAN to them all the time!"

"If you had the <u>slightest</u> interest in passing this course, you'd at least TRY to understand the ma<u>ter</u>ial."

"You <u>know</u> I'd never tell you what to DO, dear . . . but you'll reGRET IT the REST OF YOUR LIFE if you take that job!"

Do you say these things, or hear these things, day in and day out? Does this kind of language go on around you all the time, while you sit and try to mind your own business, miserable because you feel that you can't just get up and leave? Is this the kind of language that your children constantly hear and that serves as their model for dealing with conflict?

If your answer to any of these questions is yes, you are facing the problem of verbal abuse — as an abuser, as a victim, as an involved bystander, or as some combination of the three. And you are not alone. You have a *lot* of company!

Verbal abuse is *everywhere* in our society. It's in our homes and our workplaces, in our streets and our schools, in our courts and in our hospitals. It's the lifeblood of much of our media. Everywhere we go, we find verbal abuse and verbal violence. Sometimes it comes at us as curses and open insults, as ethnic or sexist epithets, or as vicious taunts. Often it takes the form of sarcasm and ridicule, or subtle putdowns claiming to be "helpful." It comes not just from strangers, but from people we feel affection and respect for. Often it comes from people who, we have good reason to believe, feel only positive emotions toward us. And sometimes, perhaps to our amazement and distress, it comes not from others but from *us*.

This isn't something to shrug off and take lightly. It's not trivial. Thanks to today's powerful computers, which allow us for the first time to examine the medical histories of hundreds of thousands of people over the course of decades, we now have four very important new pieces of information:

1. The two major risk factors for human illness and injury are *hostility* and *loneliness*.

2. People who are hostile or lonely (or both) get sick and injured more often, take longer to recover, suffer more complications during recovery, and die sooner.

3. Physical violence in this country — almost always beginning as *verbal* violence — has reached epidemic levels. For much of the male population, violence is actually the leading cause of death. For women, it is the leading cause of injury, and one of the most common causes of death.

4. Verbal abuse is *literally* dangerous to our health, in the same way that contaminated food and polluted water and toxic waste are dangerous. There's nothing "metaphorical" about this danger; it's real.

We couldn't see these patterns clearly in the past; when short-term data was all we had to analyze, they were invisible. But now that our computer technology lets us see what's *really* happening, we can no longer afford to ignore them.

Anyone can find himself or herself living in an environment where hostile language is common; where verbal abuse is taken for granted as "just part of everyday life"; and where people are convinced that every disagreement — no matter how trivial — has to be settled by a confrontation ending with a clear Winner and Loser. This kind of language environment isn't limited to areas of poverty or crime or severe hardship, the way many other problems of society are. It's as common — and as dangerous — in the most luxurious homes and the most elegant neighborhoods as it is anywhere else. The inescapable question is, then:

Why Do We Put Up with It?

We wouldn't let toxic waste pile up around us; why do we tolerate toxic *language*, day in and day out? Even when it makes us miserable? Even when we are well aware of its destructiveness?

It's not because we're stupid, or foolish, or wicked, or any of the other character flaws that come so easily to mind. There are three primary reasons for our strange tolerance, and they have little to do with our character or personality. They are the result of our *culture*, the environment of customs and beliefs that we grow up with and share with the other members of our society.

1. Since we were small children we have heard over and over the ancient myth, the one that goes, "Sticks and stones will break my bones, but *words* will never hurt me!" We've been called names when words *did* hurt us. We've been told that we were "neurotic" or we "have no sense of humor"; we've been called sissies and wimps and spoilsports and wet blankets and babies. We've watched television and movies and noticed over and over again that the highest ratings and the loudest applause go to the character with the meanest mouth. The message has been both loud and clear:

    ✦   If you feel pain as a result of other people's *words,* something is wrong with *you.* And if other people feel pain as a result of hearing *your* words, something is wrong with *them.*

2. Like fish who are unaware of the water they swim in, we tend to have little or no awareness of our *language* environment; it's just "there." The idea that language can be wholesome and pure — or contaminated and toxic — just like water and air, rarely occurs to us. Just as we used to take the rest of our environment for granted (and are now facing the grave negative consequences of that attitude), we still take our language environment for granted. We notice it only when something goes dramatically wrong. Most of the time, for most of us, it not only isn't a significant part of our lives, it's something we assume that we have no reason or motivation even to think about. There is no nationwide "linguistic ecology" movement.

3. Much of our physical environment is almost completely beyond our control as individuals. When we do become aware of our language environment (usually because it has become uncomfortable and unpleasant), we tend to assume that we're equally helpless to do anything about it. We can't do much, as individuals, to keep pollution out of our air and water, or to keep our

food supply free of pesticides and toxic chemicals. We have little choice about what's built in our neighborhoods or brought into our buildings. Even when we've knocked ourselves out doing all those things to "save the Earth," even when we know we've done our part, we find ourselves facing environmental messes created by other people and groups and governments. Misfortunes and disasters, illnesses and accidents and crises, every sort of negative experience, seem to just fall on us out of nowhere, in spite of our best efforts. In the end, it's not surprising that we begin to believe that the old despairing claim — "There's nothing I can *do!*" — is *always* true.

These three attitudes are so deeply embedded in our consciousness that they look like natural laws to us. We perceive them as obvious and logical and self-evident and "what everybody knows." There was a time when people felt the same way about the idea that the earth was flat: It was obvious, and any rational person could see that it had to be true. It turned out to be *false,* however, and we had to go through the painful process of unlearning something that had always been part of our model of reality. We now need to go through the same process with the three ideas above: They, too, are false. They must be unlearned and put behind us for good.

Words, it turns out, *can* hurt you. Feeling pain caused by words is as normal as feeling pain when you're hit with a brick; causing pain with words is just as dangerous as causing pain with a brick. But you're not helpless. You don't have to live surrounded by toxic language. There are many simple and practical things that you can do — as just one person — to keep your language environment from being a danger zone.

If we *were* helpless about language, it might make sense to ignore the language environment. It would be one of those things, like the potential for tornadoes and earthquakes, that you try to put out of your mind because nothing can be done about it. Since it's *not* like that, however, you can't afford not to be fully aware of the language around you, of its potential effects for good and for ill, and of your ability to take charge of the outcome.

This book will show you how to do two things that are critically important to your life:

1. How to establish an environment in which verbal abuse and verbal violence *almost never happen.*

2. And, when verbal abuse truly cannot be avoided, how to bring it under your control by learning to deal with it efficiently and effectively, with no loss of face for anyone involved.

No matter how bad your own language environment may seem right now, you *can* do both of those things. With the help of this book and your own knowledge of your language, you *can* put an end to verbal abuse and verbal violence in your life—one step at a time.

Your Personal Verbal Abuse Survey

It's hard to be sure you're moving in the right direction if you don't know where you're starting from. Answering the questions in this survey will help you get a clear picture of your own situation regarding verbal abuse before you go any further with this program.

Answer as completely and as accurately as you can, and put the finished pages in your verbal self-defense notebook. Doing this at the beginning establishes a baseline for you to work from and against which you can measure your progress. You may want to repeat the survey one or more times later, to bring you up to date on the changes that have taken place.

1. What are the five situations in my personal life where I most often run into verbal abuse?

   (Examples: When I talk to my teenage daughter; when my spouse has a faculty meeting; when my next-door neighbor comes over for coffee.)

2. What are the five situations *outside* my personal life where I most often run into verbal abuse?

   (Examples: When I have to buy gas at the OCS Station; when I have to do something for Tracy Smith; in my math class with Professor Lee.)

3. Who is the most verbally abusive person I have to deal with in my personal life?

4. Who is the most verbally abusive person I have to deal with outside my personal life?

5. Who is the person I'm most likely to verbally abuse in my personal life? Why?

6. Who is the person I'm most likely to verbally abuse outside my personal life? Why?

7. What is the verbal abuse situation I dread most?

8. What was the most painful verbal abuse ever directed at me?

9. How often do I usually have to deal with verbal abuse?

10. How often do I usually abuse others verbally?

11. Is there a situation in my life where I am verbally abused and I feel that the abuse is justified or excusable? What is it?

12. Is there a situation in my life where I verbally abuse someone else and I feel that the abuse is justified or excusable? What is it?

13. What is the first example that I can remember of verbal abuse directed at me?

14. What is the first example that I can remember when I verbally abused someone else?

15. What is the first example that I can remember of being distressed by verbal abuse between *other* people, when I wasn't directly involved myself?

16. What is my usual method for handling verbal abuse directed at me in my personal life?

17. What is my usual method for handling verbal abuse directed at me at work?

18. What is my usual method for handling verbal abuse directed at me anywhere other than in my personal life or at work?

19. What do I usually do when I know that someone feels I have verbally abused him or her? How do I usually handle that situation?

20. What do I usually do when I find myself caught in verbal abuse between other people, where I'm not directly involved? How do I usually handle that situation?

21. What is my definition of verbal abuse?

22. What is my definition of verbal self-defense?

23. Which of the following words and phrases would I use to describe verbal abuse?

inexcusable	unavoidable	necessary
useful	destructive	cruel
trivial	natural	just a normal part of life
exciting	challenging	wicked
sick	amusing	a nuisance

24. Which of the following phrases would I use to describe my own role with regard to verbal abuse and verbal violence?

a verbal abuser

a verbal victim

an innocent bystander, suffering the effects of *others'* abusive language

25. What are the verbal self-defense goals that matter most to me?

◆

Recognizing the Source of the Problem

I know that what causes the disorder in my life is language. Not things that "happen to" me . . . not things other people "do to" me . . . not faults I myself have or bad things I myself do . . . but language.

Scenario One

"What is THIS supposed to be?" Jerry demanded, holding his fork out in front of him like a spear. "And DON'T tell me it's a CASSerole, Charlotte — I already KNOW that!"

Charlotte Brown looked at her husband warily, recognizing the grimly controlled face, the narrowed eyes, the rigid shoulders — the body language that backed up the angry words — and then looked quickly away. *Here we go again!* she thought. Keeping her eyes on her plate, she said, "Well, it is a casserole, Jerry."

"Made of what?" He shook the fork at her. "Made of WHAT?"

"Chicken," she said, "and peas . . . some cream of chicken soup . . . parsley . . . nothing that you don't like."

Jerry laid the fork down on his plate with elaborate care and folded his arms across his chest.

"Charlotte," he said, his voice like ice at first, and then furious as he went on, "you know how I feel about coming home from a hard day's work and sitting down to eat slop. Just because you're too

LAzy to cook a decent MEAL! You KNOW what I think of that! DON'T you, Charlotte?"

Across the table, Charlotte saw seven-year-old Jessica struggling to go on eating. The child was pale and her lips were trembling. Any minute now Adam would start screaming from his highchair; at nine months, he was too little to understand, as Jessica certainly did understand, that it was important to be quiet when his father was like this.

"Please, Jerry," Charlotte said softly. "You're upsetting the kids."

"Oh, REALly?!"

"Yes. Really."

"This is <u>my</u> house, Charlotte, and <u>my</u> dinner! I work hard all day; I'm entitled to reLAX when I get home. It's not MY fault you've turned both of my KIDS into neurOTics!"

"Jerry," she said wearily, "<u>please</u> eat. There's nothing wrong with the casserole except that you're letting it get <u>cold</u>."

"I hate food that's just thrown together ANY old way, Charlotte, and YOU KNOW it! There's no exCUSE for—"

He stopped, with a sharp "DAMN it!" as Adam's screams filled the air. Flinging down his napkin, he shoved back his chair and left the room, slamming the door behind him.

In the silence that followed, punctuated only by Adam's gasping sobs, Jessica said, "Mama? What's a noorotic?"

Charlotte shook her head, raising both hands to signal *stop*.

"I don't want to talk about it, Jessica," she said. "My head aches, and talking will only make things worse. Just put it out of your mind now and eat your dinner."

"But—"

"I said <u>no</u>!" Charlotte snapped. She got up and took Adam from the highchair, hushing him against her shoulder, and carried him back to sit in her lap while they ate.

"I'm sorry, Mama," the little girl said, doggedly. "I just wish Daddy wouldn't get so <u>mad</u> . . . it makes my stomach hurt."

"I know it does," Charlotte answered, trying not to sound as miserable as she felt. "I know. But Daddy doesn't <u>mean</u> to do that, honey. He loves us very much; we have to always remember that. He just had a bad day, that's all. Now, please, sweetheart, let's be quiet and finish our dinner. Okay?"

——————————— ✦ ———————————

What's Going On Here?

The Browns are a typical American family — normal healthy people living an ordinary middle-class life. Jerry and Charlotte Brown care for each other and for their children; if asked, they would both insist that their goal is to have a good marriage and a pleasant home. But much of the time they spend together as a family is spent in scenes like that in Scenario One. Why?

Jerry's Point of View

As Jerry sees it, the bad feeling is Charlotte's fault. This baffles him. He can't figure out *why* she behaves as she does. He works hard and he works long hours, trying to provide a good life for his wife and family; it seems to him that he doesn't ask much from her in return. He likes a clean, orderly house, but he's not a fanatic about it; he wants his children well cared for and well behaved, but he doesn't expect them to be angels. He likes good meals well prepared and served, but he doesn't ask for anything fancy or exotic — just good plain food decently cooked. When he's driving home from a long day at BASS-PLUS, he looks forward to seeing Charlotte and the kids, and he has a picture in his mind of the kind of evening they'll have. In that picture they sit down to a nice meal and have relaxed and easy conversation around the table, with Jessica putting in a few words now and then so she'll learn how it's done. In that picture, he sees Charlotte clearing away the dishes, with a little help from him . . . and then they have a quiet few hours together before bedtime, to spend watching TV or reading or maybe just sitting outside watching the kids play . . . .

This, Jerry believes, is the picture of a normal family life, and he's sure that Charlotte would agree. The question is: Why can't she help him make that picture fit *their* family life? Why does she always have to do something to spoil the evening before it even gets started? Why can't she do her *part*? She knows he hates casseroles. It wouldn't have taken her more than fifteen minutes longer to cook something he would enjoy; why didn't she *do* that? Why didn't she care enough *about* him to make that small effort? It made him so angry that he couldn't keep quiet about it; he had to get it off his chest.

It seems to Jerry that his dinner (and everybody else's) is spoiled by an ugly scene at least half the time. Or if dinner goes well, the scene happens *after* dinner and ruins the evening. He feels that Charlotte must have some reason for the crazy way she behaves, some private agenda, but he absolutely cannot figure out what it is. He only knows that he resents it bitterly, and that it makes him miserable.

Charlotte's Point of View

Jerry's right that Charlotte would agree with his picture of normal family life. She wants the same things he does, exactly. But it seems to her that Jerry goes out of his way to make it impossible for them to have that kind of life. Take tonight, for example. She had intended to fry the chicken, the way she knows he likes it best, instead of putting it in a casserole. But when she got home, already running late because the traffic was terrible, she discovered that the babysitter had used the last of the shortening to make cookies for the kids. If it hadn't been Thursday — the one day of the week when she works a whole day instead of stopping at noon — she would have just gone to the store. But it *was* Thursday. As it was, she did the best she could, and she made sure that the rest of the meal was prepared as Jerry liked it. He didn't notice that, of course; he only noticed the casserole. And he didn't bother asking whether there was a *reason* for the casserole; he just blew up at her as if she'd robbed a bank.

As Charlotte sees it, Jerry is just plain *mean.* She makes excuses for him to Jessica and Adam, because she doesn't want the children to think badly of their father. But it's her opinion that he means every cruel nasty word he says, and that he enjoys the effect those words have. She feels that she and Jerry have a bad marriage, and she doesn't know what to do to make it better, either for them or for the kids.

Jessica's and Adam's Point of View

Jessica doesn't understand why her mother and father can't get along. She loves them both and she wants them to be happy. It scares her when her father yells at her mother, and it scares her when her mother doesn't seem to have any idea how to make him stop. It scares her when, as often happens, she sees her mother crying.

Whatever Adam is thinking (not something we can be very sure about when the thinker is a baby!), it's quite clear what he's *feeling*: Adam is afraid.

What Goes Wrong—And Why

Scenario One shows a type of chronic communication breakdown that is unfortunately very common; it is in fact probably the *most* common one. It's easily explained:

✦ Chronic communication breakdown happens when we don't realize that the source of a problem is language and we take it for granted that the problem is caused by a *person.*

When we hear words (and observe body language) that cause us pain, our tendency is to come to conclusions like these:

"He likes to hurt people; he went out of his way just now to hurt me."

"She doesn't like me; she doesn't think I'm good enough for her daughter."

"He said that because I'm overweight" [Or "short," or "disabled," or "Asian"].

"She said that because I drive an old car and don't make much money."

"It's my fault . . . I always do the wrong thing. No <u>wonder</u> nobody wants me around!"

"She's going to fire me . . . what am I going to <u>do</u>?"

"He's going to flunk me . . . I might as well drop out."

"Nobody's ever willing to give me an even break; they're all against me. What's the use of trying?"

"This is what happens to people like me; this is how other people treat us."

"If I'd gone to college I wouldn't be stuck with a boss who thinks it's funny to make other people look bad."

When we say words (and use body language) that cause pain for other people, and they react in ways we don't like, our tendency is to come to conclusions like these:

"She's not very bright or she'd understand that I'm only kidding."

"If he'd grown up in a decent home he wouldn't be such a wimp."

"She doesn't like me anyway, so she twists everything I say to fit the picture she has of me."

"He's so touchy . . . you have to walk on eggs all the time or he gets his feelings hurt."

"People in this part of the country just don't know how to get along with others."

"It takes a really narrow mind to find something offensive in half a dozen friendly words like I said."

PACKING SLIP:
Amazon Marketplace Item: You Can't Say That to Me: Stopping
Verbal Abuse -- An 8-Step...
Listing ID: 0402F020106
SKU:
Quantity: 1

Purchased on: 26-May-2006
Shipped by: jroxy46@yahoo.com
Shipping address:

Ship to: Kim Palmer
Address Line 1: 2113 Martin Dr
Address Line 2:
City: Medford
State/Province/Region: OR
Zip/Postal Code: 97501-8137
Country: United States

Buyer Name: Kim

"I don't know what I did to get stuck in this place where every-body else is just plain weird."

"That's how people like that act; they don't know any better."

"That's how people like him treat people like me; it makes no difference what I do, he'll turn it into something bad."

"If I were younger [or "taller" or "better looking" or "better dressed"], he wouldn't talk to me like that."

"This is just one more example that proves people are out to get you. It's a <u>jungle</u> out there!"

Every single one of these conclusions could be true.
No question about it. In the right circumstances, with evidence to back them up, they could be accurate descriptions of the real world. When they *are* accurate, when there's solid evidence to back them up, each one makes a negative reaction toward the persons they describe understandable. But most of the time we don't have any evidence — often we don't even stop to consider whether there might *be* evidence. We hear a few words or sentences that strike us as unacceptable; we observe a few items of body language that we find inappropriate; and on that basis alone we come to negative conclusions, not about the language but about the *speaker.* This is bad strategy. To avoid it, we need to keep one fact firmly in mind:

✦ There's plenty of time to be angry if anger is justified; first, look for an explanation.

That is, if we learn that our negative conclusions about the other person's character and motivation and attitudes are correct, we can deal with that information at the time and plan our behavior accordingly. But it takes only a minute or two to stop and check for an alternative explanation. Except in acute emergencies, that minute or two is always available to us. It's not that we lack the necessary language skills to do this checking. We have the skills; we just don't use them.

How many times have you said something you were certain was absolutely clear, only to find out that the person you spoke to got a completely different meaning from it than the one you intended?

How many times have you misunderstood someone else's words and body language, perhaps with consequences that caused trouble for weeks or months before you discovered that it *was* a misunderstanding?

Unless you are very unusual, a review of your own personal experience will tell you that negative conclusions like those listed on pages 13–15 are likely, much of the time, to be wrong.

This *matters*. It matters because we don't just "get in a fight" the way we might fall off a ladder or trip over a rug. FIRST, THERE IS LANGUAGE. First, words are exchanged; *then* we fight. There's time in the early stages of the language interaction to work toward a different outcome. Time to find out what the words were *really* intended to mean. Time to find out what's behind the chilly facial expression or the angry gesture. Time to isolate the word or phrase or item of body language that doesn't have the same meaning for the other person that it has for us. Time to avoid the misunderstanding, or repair it.

Here are some examples of things to say as a way of doing this linguistic investigation when the language you hear and observe seems to you to be deliberately hurtful.

"I think I must have misunderstood you. Could you say that again for me, please?"

"I wonder if the word '_____' has a different meaning for you than it does for me. What do *you* mean when you say that word?"

"That doesn't sound like you at all; I think I must have misunderstood. Please—tell me again."

"I would like very much to understand what you're saying, and I don't think I do. Let's try this again."

"I know you wouldn't have said that unless you had a good reason; could you tell me what it was?"

And here are some examples for use when the possible misunderstanding begins with someone else's reaction to *your* speech.

"I have a feeling that perhaps you misunderstood me. Let me try to be more clear."

"Your reaction is a surprise to me; I must not have made myself clear. Tell me, what did you think I meant to say?"

"When I see a reaction like yours, I feel concerned, because it usually means that I've failed to make myself clear. Could you help me understand where I went wrong?"

"I don't think I got my message across! Let's try this again."

"I know you wouldn't have reacted like that to what I said without a good reason. I'd like very much to know what it is."

Sequences like these will usually get a *negotiation of the meaning* under way for both people involved. They take only a few seconds, and they demonstrate your willingness to consider the language interaction you're involved in with an open mind instead of leaping to conclusions.

We have to stop taking it for granted that when things go badly around us it's because of the stupidity or obnoxiousness of other people, or because of the negative reactions other people have to our appearance, our education, the type of work we do, and so forth. MOST OF THE TIME, THAT'S NOT IT. Most of the time, the problem isn't our looks or our car or our briefcase, and it isn't the other person's prejudices or sadistic nature. Most of the time, the problem is language.

What to Do about It: Using Miller's Law

One of the first and most basic steps we can take to avoid misunderstanding and hostility, either in brief encounters or in chronic difficult situations, is to put into practice a rule known as *Miller's Law*.

In order to understand what another person is saying, you must assume that it is true and try to imagine what it could be true of. (G. Miller 1980, p. 46)

That is: Assume — not accept, just assume — that the other person's words are true, and try to imagine what they could be true *of*. In what kind of reality would they be true? What would be happening? What else would have to be true if they were true?

When we hear another person say something that strikes us as impossible or outrageous, our tendency is to follow what might be called *Miller's-Law-in-Reverse*. Like Miller's Law, this rule has two parts:

1. We assume that what the person said is *false*.

2. We try to imagine *what could be wrong with the person who is talking* that would account for their saying something so unacceptable to us.

Almost always, this guarantees misunderstanding, communication breakdown, and a hostile language environment.

We need to use Miller's Law instead, consciously, actively, and deliberately. Suppose it turns out that the person speaking to you really did say the outrageous utterance because he was trying to cause trouble . . . because she doesn't like you . . . because he's prejudiced against your ethnic group . . . because she hasn't bothered to do her homework . . . because he's just a mean and nasty person . . . because she is a liar. In all those instances, you'll find that out in the course of the conversation and you'll have an opportunity to deal with it appropriately. But *first*, apply Miller's Law.

When you react negatively to something another person says and go straight to Miller's-Law-in-Reverse, several things happen:

• You stop listening. Your mind is already made up, where the *language* you heard is concerned.

• Your body language immediately reflects the fact that you have rejected what was said.

- You then respond, based not on the language you heard but on your negative conclusions about *the person who spoke the words.*

All three of these things naturally cause a negative reaction in the other person. You now have a hostility loop set up and being fed from both ends.

This won't happen if you apply Miller's Law. You assume that what you heard is true, giving the other person the benefit of the doubt, and you listen with an open mind, so that you can get the information you need to verify that assumption and find out what it is true *of.*

Dialogues for Analysis

Suppose Jerry and Charlotte are at a cocktail party that's important to Jerry's business . . .

DIALOGUE ONE: *Without Miller's Law*

Charlotte: "<u>Gracious</u>, it's hot in here!"

Jerry: "Look, it <u>won't</u> <u>hurt</u> you to spend an hour with these people!"

Charlotte: "But Jerry, I — "

Jerry: "Do you want me to get this account or <u>not</u>, Charlotte? If you do, you've got to HELP me a little!"

Notice what happens here. Charlotte complains about the heat and Jerry applies Miller's-Law-In-Reverse. He decides that her statement is false, asks himself what her motive for saying it could have been, and leaps to the conclusion that she's trying to make an excuse to leave the party. He then responds to "Jerry, I don't want to stay, even if it <u>would</u> help you get the account you're working on!" — which is something Charlotte did not say.

DIALOGUE TWO: *With Miller's Law*

Charlotte: "<u>Gracious</u>, it's hot in here!"

Jerry: "Are you uncomfortable? How about if we move over by the window?"

Charlotte: "Good idea . . . There's a nice breeze, if we were just where we could <u>feel</u> it."

This time Jerry assumes that Charlotte's words are true and asks himself what they could be true of. He can think of several possibilities. Charlotte's dress might be in too heavy a fabric for the room temperature, for example. He responds to what she actually said. And he can safely conclude from her next utterance that she said she was too warm because it was in fact the truth. If she'd really been trying to get out of staying at the party, she would have said something like, "Oh, it won't make any difference <u>where</u> we're standing! I'm still going to be uncomfortable!" It takes Jerry no longer to do it this way; and he and Charlotte are far more likely to impress his business contacts than they would have been after the hostile exchange in Dialogue One.

We'll come back to the use of Miller's Law many times throughout this program. There are few things you can do that go farther to make a wholesome language environment possible than this one simple technique does.

We have to begin taking the time to do two things:

1. We must make an active effort to *remember* that the source of a communication problem usually is not a person but a sequence of language.

2. We must make an active effort to *pay attention* to language — to pay attention both to our own speech and to the speech we hear from others.

We need to train ourselves to do these two things *before* we leap to conclusions about ourselves, others, or the universe at large. If our first impulsive conclusions are accurate, we'll find that out anyway — but they may not be. We can't find out unless we stop and listen, with care and with our full attention — *and without unsupported preconceptions* — to the language we use and to the language coming at us.

Another Look at Scenario One

Both Jerry and Charlotte are at fault in the scenario, although the openly abusive language comes from Jerry. For example, when Jerry got home it would have been good strategy for Charlotte to tell him what was going to happen. Like this:

> "Jerry, I want to let you know that we're having a chicken casserole for dinner. I'm sorry about that. I won't bore you with the reasons, but I assure you they're good ones. You know I wouldn't serve something you don't like if I could avoid it."

If Jerry *wants* the reasons, he now has an opportunity to say so, and Charlotte can supply them. If he's going to be angry about the casserole in spite of her explanation, he and Charlotte can get the argument over with *before* dinner instead of at the table, which would be an improvement.

If no warning takes place, and Jerry finds himself at the table confronting a main dish he dislikes, he has many alternatives to "What is THIS supposed to be? And DON'T tell me it's a CASSerole, Charlotte — I already KNOW that!" They're not alternatives that prevent him from saying how he feels or make him sound like a wimp. Here are three examples.

- "Charlotte, we both know I really dislike casseroles. Is there a good reason for this one?"

- "Charlotte, you wouldn't have made this casserole without a good reason — I know that. I don't want to know what it was, honey, I'll take it on faith. But I really don't like casseroles."

- "Charlotte, I hate casseroles. Why are we having one?"

If the response he gets from Charlotte is something along the lines of "I made a casserole because I couldn't care <u>less</u> what you want to eat!" he still has plenty of time to fight with her about it. But we know what happened: Charlotte got home from work too late to go to the store and found herself out of the essential ingredients for anything *but* a casserole. There's no reason for a fight.

Suppose Jerry doesn't stop and offer Charlotte the opportunity to explain. There are still ways to prevent the fight without sacrificing any dignity or principles, and *all* of them are a vast improvement over her "Well, it <u>is</u> a casserole, Jerry."

Jerry says:

"What is THIS supposed to be? And DON'T tell me it's a CASSerole, Charlotte — I already KNOW <u>that</u>!"

And Charlotte can say any one of these three things:

1. "Jerry, you wouldn't be talking that way just because I made a casserole unless you had a good reason. Help me out a little — tell me why you're so angry."

2. "I wish it wasn't a casserole, too, Jerry. You and I are in complete agreement about that."

3. "The traffic was terrible and I got home from work too late to go to the store. If I had a magic wand, Jerry, we'd be eating fried chicken tonight."

It's at *this* point — at the very beginning of the exchange, before a lot of unpleasant things are said and thought — that matters can be easily set right. Jerry saw the casserole and came to an immediate negative conclusion: *It was there because Charlotte is a bad woman, lazy and indifferent to his needs.* Charlotte heard his angry words and came to an immediate negative conclusion: *Jerry is a bad man, a bully who enjoys making people miserable.*

From that point on, both Jerry and Charlotte — and their children — paid the penalty for those conclusions, both of which were in fact *false*. And when Charlotte makes excuses to the children for Jerry's language, she gives them the false message that it's *okay* to use verbal abuse if you've had a hard day. That's unfortunate; that's a good way to start bringing up children to be verbally abusive themselves. It could so easily have been avoided.

Beyond the Dinner Table

Much verbal abuse takes place in the home, but the patterns shown in Scenario One also occur in quite different situations. Look at these dialogues.

At the Office

Boss: "What is THIS supposed to be? And DON'T tell me it's a four-page memorandum — I already KNOW that!"

Employee: "Well, it is a four-page memorandum, Mr. Jones."

At the Campus

Prof: "What is THIS supposed to be? And DON'T tell me it's a handwritten term paper — I already KNOW that!"

Student: "Well, it is a handwritten term paper, Professor Lee."

Rewritten as useful communication from both speakers, the dialogues would look like this:

At the Office

Boss: "I'm sure you know how much I object to long memos. Why is this one four pages long?"

Employee: "The committee insisted that all seventeen topics had to be included, Mr. Jones. There was no way to make it shorter."

At the Campus

Prof: "I'm certain you know that all term papers have to be typed. Yours is handwritten. Would you explain, please?"

Student: "I don't know how to type, Professor Lee, and I can't afford to hire somebody else to do it. I know that's no excuse; it <u>is</u> an explanation."

Neither the employer nor the professor in these dialogues is likely to change opinions about the proper format for memos and term papers. But in both cases the listener has been given an opportunity to demonstrate that the behavior provoking the speaker was due to outside circumstances rather than deliberate malice or some other negative personal characteristic.

✦ WARNING: It's important to realize that *any words whatsoever,* including "I love you with all my heart," can be said in such a way that they are verbal abuse. That's true of all the suggested rewrites and revisions in this chapter, also. They *could* be said sarcastically, coldly, cuttingly, or worse. We'll return to the subject of *how* words are said in Step 5. For now, assume that the pleasant or neutral words written on the page *would* be said pleasantly or neutrally.

Step 1 Backup

---◆---

Hasty Conclusions Log

Set up a supply of pages in your verbal self-defense notebook as shown below, leaving as many empty lines as you feel you'll need to answer all the questions in full. Your goal for this diary page is to record three types of information:

1. The conclusions you came to when you heard someone use language that you perceived as abusive or otherwise objectionable.

2. The evidence you based your conclusions on.

3. The outcome—that is, whether you turned out to be right or wrong.

(Remember: For this and all backups, if you dislike writing you can record the information on an audiotape instead.)

DATE: _____

DESCRIPTION OF THE SITUATION

   (Where you were; why you were there; who else was there; what was going on at the time; any important details to help you remember the situation clearly later.)

MY REACTION:

When I heard _____ say "_____

_____," the conclusion I came to was

_____.

MY EVIDENCE FOR MY CONCLUSION(S):

WHAT HAPPENED—THE CONSEQUENCES:

(Later, I learned that I had been right/wrong.)

COMMENTS:

Negotiated Meanings Incident Log

Your goal for this diary page is to keep a record of what happens when you use sentences like those on pages 16–17 ("I must have misunderstood you/You must have misunderstood me" and "Let's try this again") to head off a communication breakdown.

DATE: _____

DESCRIPTION OF THE SITUATION

WHAT WAS SAID TO ME:

WHAT I SAID IN RESPONSE:

(Repeat these two lines as often as needed, to record the whole interaction.)

WHAT HAPPENED—THE CONSEQUENCES:

CONCLUSION:

(The reason that _____ and I were having trouble

communicating was _____

_____.)

COMMENTS:

Miller's Law Incident Log

For this diary page, you want to keep a record of three items of information:

1. The utterance you reacted to negatively (because it struck you as false, outrageous, impossible, etc.)

2. The response you made using Miller's Law ("In order to understand what another person is saying, you must assume that it is true and try to imagine what it could be true of.")

3. The results of the interaction.

DATE: _____

DESCRIPTION OF THE SITUATION:

WHAT THE OTHER PERSON SAID:

*THE NEGATIVE REACTION THAT I FELT BUT DIDN'T
EXPRESS:*

WHAT I SAID, APPLYING MILLER'S LAW:

(Repeat if necessary, to record all the relevant lines.)

WHAT HAPPENED—THE CONSEQUENCES:

COMMENTS:

✦ SIGHT BITES ✦
Quotations to Think About and Use

ON LISTENING AND USING MILLER'S LAW

"Sometimes I don't hear him clearly because of what I expect him to say."

(A manager, quoted in Bolton 1979, p. 72.)

"When we listen to people there is an alternating current, and this recharges us so that we never get tired of each other."

(Ueland 1992, p. 105.)

ON THE LINK BETWEEN LANGUAGE AND HEALTH

"Communication is vitally linked to our bodies and is probably the single most important force that influences our health or lack of health."

(J. Lynch, "The Broken Heart: The Psychobiology of Human Contact," in Ornstein and Swencious 1990, p. 75.)

"It is the person who sets himself apart from the social framework . . . and acts in a hostile way to others who is at risk."

(Ornstein and Sobel 1987, p. 172.)

"The tongue has the power of life and death."

(Proverbs 18:21.)

"In a person whose basic response to any situation is hostility, suspicion and a desire for control, stress hormones constantly surge through the body because everything is perceived as a threat."

("How Hostile Thinking Makes You Heart-Sick," 1989, p. 5.)

"With the discovery that cells 'talk' to each other through chemical messengers, errors in communication . . . have been found to be the common mechanism for a number of diseases."

(Justice 1987, p. 92.)

ON THE POWER OF LANGUAGE

"And the most powerful stimulus for changing a person's mind is not a chemical. It's not a shock. It's not a baseball bat. It's a *word*."

(G. Miller, quoted in "Giving Away Psychology in the 80's," in Hall 1980, p. 41.)

"If I know somebody well, in ten minutes . . . I could perhaps say to them things so cruel, so destructive, that they would never forget them for the rest of their life. But could I in ten minutes say things so beautiful, so creative, that they would never forget them?"

(Bishop Kallistos Ware, quoted in "Image and Likeness," p. 66.)

"When the other creatures of the earth come into conflict, they must either fight or run away. Our ability to communicate ideas has given us another choice. We can use our jaws for purposes other than to maim or threaten . . ."

("The Art of Negotiation," 1986, p. 1.)

✦

Recognizing the Source
of the Solution

*"I know that the only solution for a problem
caused by language is other language:
language that is more effective and works* **for** *me
instead of* **against** *me."*

Scenario Two

"Really, Charlotte!"

Charlotte turned, startled, to look at her mother-in-law. "Is something wrong, Lydia?" she asked the other woman.

Lydia's lips tightened, and her eyes narrowed. "If I have to TELL you, Charlotte," she snapped, "there are TWO things wrong! I can't beLIEVE you'd feed that baby BACon!"

Charlotte's hand stopped in midair. Adam, his mouth already wide open, looked bewildered; he had enjoyed the first bite of bacon very much and was looking forward to the second one.

"Lydia," Charlotte said carefully, "I certainly don't give him bacon very often. But once in a while, as a treat, I don't think it does him any harm. He loves bacon."

"You might as well just POISON the child and be DONE with it!"

"I don't think that's accurate," Charlotte answered, keeping her voice as polite as possible. "According to current research, human beings need a certain amount of fat in their diet. In fact, unless people get at least—"

"You may be a NURSE, Charlotte," Lydia said, cutting her off, "but I am not TOTALLY ignorant!"

"Lydia, I didn't mean to imply — "

"Oh, I think you DID! It was very clear to ME, Charlotte, that you felt obligated to EDUCATE me! But I'm not surprised, you know. I've noticed many times that when a wife and mother decides to go out to work instead of devoting herself to her house and children, it's because she feels a need to demonstrate her <u>superiority</u> to other <u>people</u>."

Charlotte bit her lip, took a deep breath, and gave the baby the rest of the piece of bacon she was holding in her hand. *Not* this *time!* she thought. *I am absolutely not going to get suckered into another argument with her about quitting my job!*

"<u>I</u> always stayed HOME with MY children," Lydia went on. "I always felt that no job on earth was as important, or as ful<u>fill</u>ing, as making a home for my husband and taking care of my children <u>myself</u>. And I think these modern women who put their personal whims ahead of the welfare of their families are going to be VERY SORRY one day, when they start reaping the CONsequences!"

It was too much; it was more than Charlotte could bear.

"Mother Brown," she said, her voice trembling with outrage, "I do NOT put my 'whims,' as you put it, ahead of my family!" *There is a limit,* she thought, *to the abuse I am willing to take from her.*

"I never said you <u>did</u>, dear," Lydia answered sweetly. "I hope I have sense enough to mind my own business and keep my opinions to myself." And she went over to the highchair to chuck Adam under the chin. "Aren't you a HANDSOME boy!" she declared.

Charlotte stood there with her heart pounding and her fists clenched; she was *amazed* at how much she would have liked to hit her mother-in-law over the head. The woman was *impossible!*

◆

What's Going On Here?

Lydia's Point of View

Lydia Brown is a woman in her fifties who has never worked outside her home. She is dedicated exclusively to her role of homemaker and mother, and always has been; she disapproves in the strongest terms of any married woman who works when her financial situation doesn't force her to do so. She knows her son's salary isn't large, but she is convinced that the family could manage without a second income if Charlotte would only make an effort — if she would learn to sew, if she would keep a sizable garden and put the food by, if she would just do the things that Lydia herself always did to make ends meet. It's obvious to her that Charlotte knows she shouldn't work, even though she won't admit it; the fact that she works only part-time is clear proof of that.

If Lydia had the authority to simply *order* Charlotte to give up her job, she'd do it; she's sure that although the younger woman would resent it at first, she would soon realize that Lydia had been right all along. Lacking the authority to give such an order, she considers it her duty to Jerry and Jessica and Adam to keep up a steady constant pressure on Charlotte until she gives in. She realizes that this makes Charlotte dread her company, and she resents that very much. After all, Charlotte is the one responsible for the problem; she could put an end to the disagreement at any time just by admitting that she's wrong. It seems to Lydia that her daughter-in-law should have sense enough to appreciate the wealth of experience she is willing to share; it seems to her that Charlotte should be grateful that Lydia loves them all enough to keep on trying to do what's best for them, even in the face of stubbornness and arrogance.

Charlotte's Point of View

As Charlotte perceives it, Lydia is a domineering narrow-minded woman whose behavior demonstrates vividly where martyring yourself in the homemaker role leads. Charlotte enjoys looking after her house and family, but she also enjoys working; it seems to her that as long as she's careful to neglect neither home nor work she has the right to do both. It seems to her that limiting herself to a part-time job is proof enough that she puts her family first. And she is 100 percent certain that if she *did* neglect Jerry and the kids, they'd still be better off than if Charlotte stayed home and turned into a cruel and thoughtless uncaring woman like Lydia.

Charlotte tries hard to win her mother-in-law over, because she knows their failure to get along hurts Jerry. But nothing she does is ever enough, and no matter how carefully she tries to explain her reasons for the choices she makes, she gets nowhere. Charlotte doesn't intend to give up; she will keep trying for her family's sake. She doesn't think there's much hope, however — because Lydia refuses even to *listen*.

◆

These two women have a great deal in common. Both are devoted to their families; both are hardworking and competent and intelligent; both love Jerry and Jessica and Adam and want them to be happy. It seems absurd that they can't learn to get along together, because they share so many interests and goals. But as the scenario shows, things are very bad between them.

Charlotte and Lydia have a problem that is common in small groups of any kind: *Even when they agree on the facts, they* interpret *them very differently; and they have no idea that that difference exists.* For example: They both agree that Charlotte's working only part-time is significant. But while Charlotte believes it proves that her family comes first with her, Lydia believes it proves that Charlotte feels guilty about working at all. And neither woman is aware of this substantial difference in their perceptions.

This isn't just a matter of an occasional argument in heated moments. Whenever the two women are together, Lydia actively pursues her campaign to make Charlotte into a better wife and mother, while Charlotte actively resists her efforts. They are a classic verbal abuser/verbal victim pair.

The Basics—Defining Our Terms

Anybody can become verbally abusive, or become a verbal victim, once in a while — in a crisis, or because some unusual factor like exhaustion or illness is interfering with their usual language behavior. Anyone can become indirectly involved in a verbal confrontation by accident, just by being in the wrong place at the wrong time and not feeling free to leave the scene. When we use the terms *verbal abuser* and *verbal victim*, we're not talking about that kind of occasional and untypical behavior, and we can set it aside. We're talking about people who use verbal abuse or are subjected to verbal abuse, *frequently and consistently,* in at least one life situation.

Someone who never uses verbal abuse in the workplace but consistently does so at home (or vice versa) is a verbal abuser. Someone who would not tolerate verbal abuse at home but who consistently takes it without protest at work (or vice versa) is a verbal victim. Someone who is regularly and consistently surrounded by the verbal abuse of others and seems locked into that role is a verbal victim of a different kind, for which we have no appropriate English word. For lack of a better term, we'll call such people "involved bystanders." Some people fill two or more of these roles, depending on where they are and who they're with; others fill only one.

The phenomenon of verbal abuse is complicated, and is sadly neglected in our society even by those who claim to deplore it. We don't learn about it in school; it gets very little attention in our media. It doesn't have the evil glamour that physical abuse has; it doesn't make headlines. When it does get attention, the information is usually sensationalized or distorted, or both. We need to repair this information shortfall. Let's stop and discuss typical verbal abusers and victims — people who are *chronically* involved in verbal abuse — with particular focus on *why* they behave as they do. We can't identify them by physical characteristics or demographics; they can't be recognized by the color of their eyes or where they live or what they do for a living. *Except in the way they use language, verbal abusers and their victims are just like everybody else.*

The English word "why" has two meanings (often assigned to two separate words in other languages):

1. There is the "why" that asks for a reason, as in "Why are you leaving?"/"Because I'm tired."

2. There is the "why" that asks for a *purpose,* as in "Why are you leaving?"/"So that I can beat the rush hour traffic and get home by six." In very formal speech this "why" is often paired with "in order to," as in "Why are you transferring the funds?"/"In order to meet my obligations to the IRS."

It's important to keep this distinction carefully in mind. Our concern here is with the second meaning of the word: We want to discuss the *purposes* that verbal abuse serves in people's lives.

The Verbal Abuser

In normal conversation, people ask questions in order to get responses, and they want those responses to contain the information that *answers* their questions. In normal conversation, people introduce topics in order to get responses that are appropriate to the situation and that will make it possible to continue discussing those topics. There may be a variety of other conversational goals associated with the questions or statements — to make a promise, to give comfort, to explain or instruct or apologize, to pass the time, to show affection, and so forth — but the conditions just stated hold true.

Verbal abuse may look like normal conversation at first glance and sound like it at first hearing, but there is a critical difference:

◆ Verbal abusers are not interested in the answers to their questions or responses to their statements that would be expected in other circumstances. They're not interested, other than coincidentally, in the issues they raise.

That is: Verbal abusers say the things they say for purposes that are quite different from the purposes typical of normal conversation.

People who consistently use verbal abuse are interested in just two things:

1. A demonstration of their power to get and keep the *attention* of the person they're speaking to.

2. The emotional reaction they are able to provoke in the person they're speaking to, which is additional evidence demonstrating their power.

This doesn't mean that verbal abusers are *consciously aware* of these two goals. On the contrary. If asked to explain their language behavior in a situation of verbal abuse, they will give explanations like these:

- "It's for his own good."
- "It's because I have to make her understand what she has to do."
- "It's because I love him so much and I want him to do well."
- "It's because she's stubborn and refuses to cooperate."
- "It's because I'm in charge here and it's important for them to treat me with respect."
- "It's because she goes out of her way to provoke me, and she has to be taught not to do that."
- "It's because I was brought up to believe that this is how a home [or "a business" or "a class"] is <u>supposed</u> to be run."
- "It's because he's my <u>child</u>." (Or "she's my <u>wife</u>.")
- "It's because <u>some</u>body has to be in <u>charge</u>."

Such claims may well be accurate descriptions of the situation; the abuser may honestly have the attitudes, motives, and goals expressed. However, one fact is being ignored:

✦ There is always a way to achieve the same communication goal *without* using abusive language.

In Scenario Two, Lydia Brown could say with complete honesty that she loves her son and his family, that she believes their welfare requires her daughter-in-law to be a full-time homemaker and mother, and that her purpose is to achieve that goal for those she loves. This is the truth. What's *false* is the idea that the only language available to Lydia for achieving her goal is hostile and abusive language.

In the real world, people *do* exist who use verbal abuse to work toward a goal because they know physical force is unacceptable or inappropriate, but they don't know that any nonabusive *verbal* method exists. This isn't the usual situation, but it does happen.

People like this, whose verbal abuse is due only to ignorance, will make an effort to change their ways when they realize that they have alternatives. All they need is information, such as the information provided in this book, and some practice in putting it to use. But these are not typical verbal abusers. The typical verbal abuser *knows* that alternatives exist, but chooses verbal abuse instead (not necessarily at the level of conscious awareness).

What both kinds of verbal abusers have in common, and what we have to make a conscious effort to remember, is this:

✦ They don't use verbal abuse for the purpose of causing pain.

That is, the fact that someone is a verbal abuser does not mean that he or she is a sadistic person who takes pleasure in the suffering of others. Certainly sadistic people, cruel people, mean people, do exist; certainly such people will use verbal abuse as one of their methods for inflicting pain. But it does not follow from the fact that sadistic people use verbal abuse that people who use verbal abuse are therefore sadistic.

Suppose you know five men who are over six feet tall and are cruel. You wouldn't conclude from this sample that all, or even many, men over six feet tall are cruel. In the same way, the fact that you know five men who are both verbally abusive and cruel doesn't mean that all, or even many, male verbal abusers are cruel. The correlation is a coincidence.

We can safely say that verbal abusers fall into three broad groups within which we find the same sort of individual variation that we find in any other group of human beings. Here are the three groups:

✦ *Group One:* People who use verbal abuse to achieve the two goals already discussed: (1) demonstrating their power to get and keep the victim's attention and (2) evoking an emotional response in the victim as additional evidence of that power.

This is the largest group of verbal abusers and the most common source of verbal abuse in our society. For these people, change comes in two forms: from learning that the needs filled by achieving their two goals can be satisfied in other, less destructive ways; and from the opportunity to interact with people who consistently refuse to serve as verbal victims.

✦ *Group Two:* People who use verbal abuse because they're unaware that any other method for dealing with tension and conflict is available to them.

This group is growing larger, unfortunately. Often these verbal abusers have grown up in homes where verbal abuse was essentially the only kind of communication they had as a model, especially in situations of disagreement. For them, change comes from learning better language strategies and is primarily a matter of filling information gaps and being willing to put the new information to use.

✦ *Group Three:* People whose verbal abuse is the result of a genuine psychological problem, an emotional or physical disorder, an unresolved traumatic experience in their past, or something of that kind.

For many of these people, meaningful change is possible only when the underlying problem has been solved. This may require expert help from a counselor, spiritual adviser, physician, or therapist. The majority of verbal abusers do not fall into this group. For those who do, learning communication techniques that reduce the level of tension and hostility in their language environment is helpful, even though it's not the solution to their other problem.

The Verbal Victim

Participating verbal victims do have one identifying characteristic: A great deal of the time, they're *miserable.* Without exception they are miserable during confrontations, while they are filling the victim role. And often they are miserable even when verbal abuse isn't going on, because their lives are affected so drastically and so negatively by the chronic abuse.

Unlike verbal abusers, the majority of verbal victims are genuinely unaware of their options. They know that the verbal abuse they are hearing hurts, and they know they want the pain to stop. But they're in a difficult situation, for two primary reasons:

1. They have to deal with the fact that our society supports the ancient "Sticks and stones will break my bones, but *words* will never hurt me!" myth. They've always heard that people have no *right* to be hurt by words, that such pain is not legitimate, and that those who feel it are at fault in some way. This adds to their discomfort by imposing the additional burden of *guilt*.

2. Our culture traditionally teaches us just three ways to handle verbal abuse. They are:

    a. *Counterattacking* — being abusive in return. In addition to responding with verbal abuse of your own, this includes such actions as walking out on the abuser, refusing to answer, ignoring the abuse, and the like. All of these actions are punitive; all convey negative messages.

    b. *Pleading* — using emotional appeals to try to get the abuser to stop the abuse.

    c. *Debating* — trying to *reason* with the verbal abuser by logical arguments, statistics, presentation of factual evidence, and so forth.

None of these three methods is any help with chronic verbal abusers. Counterattacking, pleading, and debating have legitimate uses and purposes in human communication, but they're not effective as methods for handling verbal abuse. *All three methods* reward *verbal abusers by making it possible for them to achieve their goals.*

Remember: The verbal abuser's purpose is to get and keep the victim's attention, accompanied by an emotional reaction that serves as additional evidence of power over the victim. The abuser doesn't *care* what form the victim's attention and emotional response take. From the abuser's point of view, counterattacking is a fine response. Pleading is excellent. Debating (especially if the debater is able to remain cool and calm) is not quite as satisfactory. But because it's usually easy to keep a debate going for a substantial period of time, it's still acceptable; it fills the abuser's need to get and hold the victim's *attention*.

✦ Verbal victims, therefore, are ordinarily people who are doing their best to put an end to behavior that causes them pain, using strategies that are never going to work, and feeling guilty the whole time.

This weights the odds so heavily against them that failure — and more guilt — are almost inevitable.

In the same way that verbally abusive persons cannot be assumed to be sadists who take pleasure in others' pain, verbal victims cannot be assumed to be masochists who enjoy being hurt. Certainly masochists are likely to serve as verbal victims, but there's no meaningful correlation between the two. Verbal victims are trying to *avoid* pain, but are drastically handicapped in their efforts, in two ways:

1. By their feeling that they should be *ashamed* of their pain.

2. By their use of ineffective language strategies.

Involved Bystanders as Verbal Victims

Finally, there are victims who aren't functioning as a member of an abuser/victim pair and are taking no direct part in the confrontation, but who still suffer the negative effects of chronic hostility in their language environment. When this happens frequently and consistently, rather than by accident, it usually means that they are present *as an audience for the abuser, as a witness for the victim, or both.* They are there not for their *own* purposes, but for the purposes of other people.

Sometimes these victims are powerless to do anything *but* serve the purposes of the abuser or direct victim. They're afraid of what those individuals would do to them if they left the scene and are afraid to take active steps of any other kind. This is the sad situation of children whose parents regularly carry on a verbal abuser/verbal victim duet in front of them. This book is not addressed to children; but parents reading it will realize that a constant input of hostile language is dangerous, and are likely to make an effort to change their ways.

Children—even children who work hard to avoid talking like their parents—learn their *language strategies* from the models around them as they grow up. When verbal abuse is a frequent part of the model in the home, it becomes a kind of inheritance down through the generations, because the little bystanders so often grow up to be adult verbal abusers and verbal victims. Jerry Brown's behavior—with Lydia as his childhood model for handling conflict—is a good example of this unfortunate pattern.

Adults who are trapped in a job they can't risk losing may also feel forced to serve as involved bystanders for others in the workplace, especially those who outrank them. They're not as helpless as the children, however, and there are three ways in which improving their language behavior will help them solve this problem:

1. The better their verbal skills, the less likely they are to be trapped in a job where they feel more like prisoners than employees.

2. The better their verbal skills, the less likely it is that verbal abusers will find them suitable as an audience.

3. The better their verbal skills, the less likely it is that verbal victims can pressure them to stick around and serve as witnesses.

We have a label in our society for people who enjoy watching others hurt and be hurt—they are *voyeurs*, taking vicarious pleasure in violence. But again, although such people may well hang around a verbal abuser–verbal victim pair the way they would hang around the scene of an automobile accident or a fire, there is no correlation between the two behaviors except coincidentally. Bystander victims are involved in the verbal abuse not because they enjoy it but because, for one reason or another, they don't know how to avoid it. Their goal, like that of direct verbal victims, is to avoid the pain. Unfortunately, just being a passive observer and "staying out of it" isn't an effective way to achieve that goal.

Verbal victims and involved bystanders, like verbal abusers, fall into the three groups described on pages 38–39: Those whose language behavior meets a personal and largely social need; those whose language behavior results from a lack of information and from poor models; and those whose language behavior reflects a separate underlying physical, emotional, or psychological disorder requiring expert help.

✦ It will now be clear to you that if verbal abusers and victims *were* behaving as they do because of meanness or weakness or perversity, it might make sense to find ways of dealing with those negative characteristics. Since they're not, it makes no sense whatsoever.

Suppose a particular verbal abuser or victim we interact with is, coincidentally, also someone who enjoys causing or feeling pain. We will find that out over time, and we will then have to decide how we want to deal with *that* problem. But that's an entirely separate issue, and a different subject entirely. The proper strategy, until evidence to the contrary comes along, is always to assume that the problem is *not* the other person's character but a misguided use of language.

What to Do about It: Awareness

If You're a Verbal Abuser

When you start a verbal confrontation, you are setting up one end of a verbal violence loop. The first requirement for getting this pattern out of your life is *awareness*. You have to become *actively* aware of the following facts:

1. If you succeed in establishing that loop, you will cause your victim to feel pain, in just the same way that you would cause pain if you hit the person with your fist.

2. You are responsible for the pain you cause your victim. Whether the victim really is "neurotic" or "a sissy" or any of the other labels of that kind is irrelevant; the pain is your responsibility.

3. Your intentions are also irrelevant. That is, it's true that you aren't using abusive language with the intention of causing pain. When you say, "Hey, I didn't <u>mean</u> to hurt you!" or "I was <u>only</u> kidding <u>around</u>!," you're telling the truth. But that's irrelevant. *Once you know that the effect of your language is pain for your victim, lack of intent ceases to be an excuse.*

4. There are other ways—involving no verbal abuse—to achieve your goals.

If You're a Verbal Victim

When you counterattack by returning verbal abuse, when you plead with your attacker to stop, or when you debate your attacker with logical arguments and reasoning, you are setting up the *other* end of the verbal violence loop. These traditional tactics make it possible for abusers to keep the loop going, achieve their goals, and fill their needs. You need to become *actively* aware of the following facts:

1. No verbal abuser can achieve the goals of verbal abuse without the *participation* of a verbal victim.

2. Because it takes both abuser and victim to carry out verbal abuse, the victim shares some of the responsibility for what happens. The intended victim is *not* helpless.

3. There are other ways—that don't involve pleading or debating or counterattacking—to achieve your goal of putting an end to the hurtful language behavior.

4. The only way to deal effectively with verbal abuse is to use language (including body language) to make it absolutely clear that you will not serve as a verbal victim—without loss of face either for you or for your attacker.

If You're an Involved Bystander

You need information: You need the facts about verbal abuse and verbal self-defense. You need information that will let you improve your language skills so that you aren't trapped in *other* people's verbal violence loops. While you're acquiring that information by working through this eight-step program, the most important thing for you to be aware of is that *there* is *a way out. Keep that in mind, and don't give up.*

The Metaprinciple for Verbal Self-Defense

For anyone involved in verbal abuse, in any role, this simple metaprinciple holds true and must always be remembered:

◆ ANYTHING YOU FEED WILL GROW.

We would predict grave consequences for anyone who ignored this principle when taking care of children or pets or crops, but we all too often forget about it in our language interactions. It's just as true when we're *talking* with other people as it is when we're supervising their diets. Feeding the verbal abuse habit guarantees that it will grow: It will become more frequent, more hurtful, and more intense.

◆ When we initiate verbal abuse and keep it going, we're feeding it. When we respond to verbal abuse by counterattacking, pleading, or debating, we're feeding it. When we sit by as an audience or witness to verbal abuse, our presence feeds it, even if we are taking no active part in what's going on.

Finally, when we deal with verbal violence by using *physical* violence (or a substitute for physical force such as abruptly firing someone from a job, taking away their privileges, etc.), we are *still* feeding the loop. The verbal abuser may "lose" in the usual sense, and our action may solve the short-term problem. But the abuser has still been able to demonstrate the power to get our attention and to upset us; for the verbal abuser, *this is still winning.* It will do nothing at all to convince him or her to behave differently.

Now we have clear definitions and descriptions of verbal abusers, verbal victims, and *indirect* verbal victims: the involved bystanders in confrontations. One basic term — the concept of a *linguistic technique* — may still need clarification. *A linguistic technique is a specific pattern of language* behavior *that can be used deliberately and systematically as part of a communication strategy.* Miller's Law is one such technique, and a rather complicated one. For comparison and contrast, let's look at a very simple pattern called the Boring Baroque Response, which is part of a larger technique that we will return to in Step 6.

Using the Boring Baroque Response

Verbal abusers select verbal victims on the assumption that they will accept that role; the persons selected need to make it clear to the abusers that they're *wrong.* One way to do that is just to say straight out: "I refuse to play the verbal victim role for you; you're wasting your time." When that's safe and appropriate, there is no better choice. However, we often find ourselves under verbal attack by people we can't speak to so directly. The attacker may be a much older person, or someone who outranks us drastically, or someone we have good reason to fear. The attacker may be someone we know so little about that caution is advisable. Furthermore, a great deal of the time a straightforward and open refusal would cause the attacker to lose face, and that is always an undesirable outcome. Whatever the reason, when a direct "I won't do it" isn't a good choice, the Boring Baroque Response (BBR) is one useful alternative.

BBRs work because the English question word "why" *presupposes* a number of messages, including these three:

1. "You have an item of information that I want."

2. "I'm asking you to provide me with that information."

3. "I have the right to make that request of you."

To say that these messages are presuppositions means that native speakers of English know they are part of the meaning of "why," whether they are openly expressed or not; presupposed information is information that can be taken for granted. When we tell people that we have "stopped" doing something, we don't have to explain to them that at some earlier point we *started* doing it. If they speak English, we can be sure in advance that they know "start to do X" is presupposed by "stop doing X."

In normal conversation, people who ask you "why" are at least mildly interested in your answer to their question. Otherwise, they wouldn't ask. But in verbal abuse, you will remember, the questioners *aren't* interested in the responses that would be expected in ordinary conversation, and the usual presuppositions become irrelevant. When verbal abusers ask questions that begin with a strongly emphasized "WHY," they add one more presupposition to the set above, and it *is* directly relevant:

4. "You might as well not <u>bother</u> answering the question, because no matter <u>what</u> your answer is, it's not <u>good</u> enough."

By ignoring Presupposition #4 and responding directly to the presupposition that they actually want the question answered, you can refuse to play the victim role—without any need to state your refusal directly. For example:

Attack: "WHY can't you EVer do ANYthing RIGHT?"

BORING BAROQUE RESPONSE ONE:

"I think it's because of something that happened to me when I was just a little kid. We were living in Indianapolis at the time . . . No, wait! It couldn't have been Indianapolis, because that was the year my Aunt Evelyn came to visit us and brought her dog with her. So it must have been while we were living in Atlanta. Anyway, we were . . . ."

—or—

BORING BAROQUE RESPONSE TWO:

"You know, there's a lot of research on human error, and some of it is really fascinating stuff. Why, only the other day, I saw an article in the *Times* . . . No. Wait a minute. It couldn't have been the

Times, because that was the day Jane Haycraft got to the paper first and I didn't see it until almost four o'clock. It must have been in the *Tribune.* At any rate . . ."

Such responses transmit a metamessage (a message *about* a message) that can be summarized like this:

"I notice that you want my attention. All right. Here it is. But I want you to understand that getting my attention isn't going to be interesting. *It's going to be boring beyond description.*"

It's true that BBRs, like debating, can go on for quite a while. But instead of demonstrating the abuser's power to get and keep the victim's attention, they hold the abuser in limbo with an excruciatingly boring monologue. And instead of an emotional response to the content of the *attack,* the intended victim provides only whatever emotion he or she feels about the content of the boring *monologue.* The abuser can (and usually does) interrupt quickly with "Oh, never mind!," followed by leaving or changing the subject.

If the abuser is stubborn, he or she may start a new attack the first time you draw a breath. Nevertheless, the *first* attack is over, and it has *failed.*

BBRs don't reward verbal abusers, because listening to them is an unpleasant ordeal. On the other hand, they can't be interpreted as counterattacks or debating or pleading. They don't back verbal abusers into corners where they will feel obligated to respond defensively to avoid losing face. In a situation where saying "I won't do what you want" would be like throwing gasoline on a fire, using a BBR is like throwing a thick blanket over it instead. You're not *feeding* the flames, you're *smothering* them. Gently.

If you are the intended verbal victim:

It's very important *never* to say a Boring Baroque Response sarcastically, or teasingly, or with a smirk on your face! For BBRs to work they must be said neutrally; if you don't feel that you can manage to do that, don't use them. Said emotionally, they're not boring; they cease to *be* BBRs and become counterattacks. It's also important to make them no longer than is absolutely necessary for transmitting their message. BBRs kept going longer than that are a way to *punish* the verbal abuser; that's not what they're for.

If you are the verbal abuser:

When you start a verbal attack and the answer you get is a Boring Baroque Response, remember that BBRs are intended to defuse your attack courteously and considerately. They are intended to demonstrate to you that although your potential victim refuses to participate in the confrontation you had planned, he or she doesn't want to cause you distress and has no desire to make you lose face or look foolish. Keep this in mind, and make a genuine effort not to react with anger. Remember: *Verbal abuse is dangerous to* your *health.* It's just as dangerous for you as for your target. A person who makes it possible for you to *avoid* participating in an episode of hostile language is helping you, not hurting you.

If you are the involved bystander:

Be glad the intended direct victim of the attack has the skill to respond with a Boring Baroque Response. Much of the time, it will put an end to the hostility; the verbal abuser will give up. Your best move is to stay out of the way and let the intended victim handle it. Don't try to take part; don't try to help. And above all, keep your own body language carefully neutral. If you let your face or body show that you're pleased to see the abuser fail, you'll introduce *new* hostility into the situation.

Now we have a shared set of basic definitions to work with. And with that foundation, we can now take . . .

Another Look at Scenario Two

Obviously Charlotte knows her mother-in-law is trying to provoke her into confrontations, but she seems unable to resist. If she and Lydia were on good terms she might be able to insist that they discuss this pattern, and in the course of the discussion she could perhaps just say openly that she won't serve as verbal victim any longer. But she has several reasons not to use that strategy.

1. She and Lydia are on very *bad* terms; a discussion between them would be hard to control and might only make matters worse.

2. Charlotte has no reason to think she'll be able to follow *through* if she says openly that she won't play victim any more. Her track record in this regard is terrible.

3. Lydia is an older woman and the mother of Charlotte's husband. In our culture, this means Charlotte is expected to speak to her with respect and courtesy, whether Lydia appears to deserve that or not. To say, "I won't be your verbal victim any longer, Lydia" is also to say, "Lydia, you are a verbal abuser who keeps attacking me — shame on you." Doing that with respect and courtesy would take great skill, and if it went wrong it would provide Lydia with ammunition for many *new* attacks on Charlotte in the future.

When Lydia attacked with "I can't beLIEVE you'd feed that baby BACon!" Charlotte tried to respond with logical arguments. Suppose she had been familiar with the Boring Baroque Response . . . the dialogue could then be rewritten like this:

Lydia: "I can't beLIEVE you'd feed that baby BACon!"

Charlotte: "Isn't it amazing the way ideas about feeding babies keep changing? They can't even agree on whether it's better to breastfeed a baby or use formula! I saw an article last week in *Family Circle* where the writer claimed that . . . Oh. No, wait a minute! It wasn't in *Family Circle,* Lydia, it was in — "

Lydia: "Oh, for heaven's sakes, Charlotte! Never <u>mind</u>!"

A stranger might wait longer to interrupt, and might interrupt less rudely — perhaps by saying, "That's interesting. I'm sorry I can't stay while you tell me the rest of it, but I really have to leave." Because Lydia spends a lot of time around Charlotte and has a long-standing bad relationship with her, the rude response is probable. However, Lydia's attack in the exchange above has failed. That's an improvement! Charlotte hasn't said anything that Lydia can use against her, and she has accomplished three useful things:

1. She has supported Lydia's topic — what to feed a baby.

2. She has said nothing disrespectful or discourteous.

3. At the same time, she has refused to accept the verbal victim role.

If Charlotte continues to defuse Lydia's attacks in this way — instead of pleading, debating, or counterattacking — Lydia will eventually give them up.

This won't happen overnight; you can't repair the damage of years in twenty-four hours. But every time Charlotte refuses to feed the verbal violence loops Lydia tries to set up, she will make herself less appealing as a verbal victim. In time, Lydia will either have to stop talking to Charlotte at all — a difficult thing to bring off within a family — or start using genuine conversation instead of verbal abuse.

✦ NOTE: Sometimes people tell me that they badly want to know the answer to the other meaning of "why." They want to know the *reason* why they use language patterns that guarantee hostile language, rather than just knowing their purposes in using them. If you feel this way and you don't feel confident that you can answer the question on your own, you might consider asking a counselor or therapist to help you with the task; it's often very hard to discover such things alone. You might also consider keeping a personal diary as a way to find the answer(s) you're seeking. Two excellent sources for this are *The New Diary* by Tristan Rainer and the writings and workshops of Ira Progoff.

Step 2 Backup

♦

Boring Baroque Response Log
(For Verbal Victims or Involved Bystanders)

Your goal for this diary page is to keep a useful record of what *happens* when a verbal attack is answered with a Boring Baroque Response, either by you or by someone else.

DATE: _____

DESCRIPTION OF THE SITUATION:

WHAT THE VERBAL ABUSER SAID:

THE BORING BAROQUE RESPONSE:

WHAT WAS SAID NEXT:

WHAT HAPPENED—THE CONSEQUENCES:

COMMENTS:

Hasty Predictions Incident Log

Remember the quotation in the Step 1 "Sight Bites" section, where a man said, "Sometimes I don't hear him clearly because of what I expect him to say"? When we make up our minds about what someone will say, we're making a hasty prediction—but even if we're wrong, it may keep us from understanding what we hear. Worse yet, it may keep us from saying things only because "I already know what he or she would say; it's no use." The goal of this diary page is to help you track your accuracy in predicting what other people will say *in response to things* you *say.*

DATE: _____

DESCRIPTION OF THE SITUATION:

MY PREDICTION:

(I knew that if I said, "_____

_____," he/she would say, "_____

_____.")

WHAT HE/SHE ACTUALLY DID SAY:

(I was right. He said, "_____

_____." Or I was wrong. She said, "_____

_____.")

COMMENTS:

✦ SIGHT BITES ✦
Quotations to Think About and Use

ON HASTY EXPECTATIONS

"The driving force behind hostility is a cynical mistrust of others. Expecting that others will mistreat us, we are on the lookout for their bad behavior — and we can usually find it."

(Williams 1989, p. 26.)

ON THE DANGERS OF HOSTILE AND ABUSIVE LANGUAGE

"The potential negative consequences of aggression . . . include fear, the provocation of counteraggression, loss of control, guilt, dehumanization, alienation from people, ill health, and the creation of a society that is too dangerous even for the aggressive to live in comfortably and safely."

(Bolton 1979, p. 132.)

"From the vantage point of the physically-battered individual, the life of anyone not in danger of being beaten probably sounds like a dream come true. But it may be just a different kind of nightmare."

(Milstead 1985, p. 34.)

"There is no cause of death that does not kill people who are lonely at significantly higher rates than those who had satisfying lives with others."

(J. Lynch, "The Broken Heart: The Psychobiology of Human Contact," in Ornstein and Swencious 1990, p. 77.)

"Prospective studies, which control for baseline health status, consistently show increased risk of death among persons with a low quantity, and sometimes low quality, of social relationships."

(House et al. 1988, p. 540.)

"A soft answer turneth away wrath: but grievous words stir up anger."

(Proverbs 15:1.)

ON LANGUAGE AND THE FAMILY

"Your most influential instructors were probably your parents, who in turn learned their approach to communication from their parents."

(Bolton 1979, p. 6.)

"Within the family, the pattern of emotional abuse is usually passed down from one generation to the next."

— and —

"Many parents are simply unfamiliar with any other method of discipline, often believing they are OK as long as they don't hit their kids. They are *not*: Experts say that belittlement, denigration, and other forms of verbal assault on children are not only cruel but also ineffective ways to teach good behavior."

(Seligman et al. 1988, p. 48.)

(Of a husband and wife.) "One day she was able to prove to him conclusively that he was factually wrong, and he replied, 'Well, you may be right, but you are wrong *because you are arguing with me.*'"

(Watzlawick 1967, p. 81.)

♦

Recognizing That You Already Have Everything You Need to Put an End to Verbal Violence in Your Life

I know that I am **not** *helpless against verbal abuse; I know that I am able to solve this language problem* **myself.** *I don't need fancy experts. All I need are two resources that are already mine in abundance: the flawless grammar of my native language that has been mine since childhood, and my own reliable common sense.**

─────────── Scenario Three ───────────

The minute Jerry walked through the door, Charlotte could tell that he was furious. She braced herself and waited for the explosion, glad that Adam was asleep and Jessica was outside playing. She didn't have to wait long.

*You may prefer one of these variations:
"All I need are two resources that God (or *Buddha,* or *the Great Spirit,* or *a Higher Power*) has given me in abundance: the flawless grammar of my native language that has been mine since childhood, and my own reliable common sense."

Jerry slammed his briefcase down on the coffee table and threw the newspaper he was carrying across the room. "Dammit, Charlotte!" he said, "What's the MATTER with you, ANYway, giving Adam BACon? You're supposed to KNOW something about feeding kids, RIGHT? Listen—EVen JESSica would know better than to load a baby up with SALT and FAT!"

Charlotte stared at him, tight-lipped, saying nothing.

"Well, Charlotte?" Jerry demanded. "I'm TALKING to you!"

She raised her eyebrows. "I noticed that," she said. "I'll go start dinner."

"Stop igNORing me, Charlotte!"

"I'm not the maid," she said coldly. "And I'm not your mother's servant, either!" She headed for the kitchen, with Jerry close on her heels.

"You'd better be grateful that my mother cares enough ABOUT us to TELL me when you act like an idiot!" he said fiercely. "GOD KNOWS what you'd do if there wasn't somebody to CHECK UP on you once in a while!"

Your mother is a tattletale and a sneak and a troublemaker, Charlotte thought, keeping her eyes firmly on the potatoes she was peeling at the sink.

"Charlotte?"

"Yes?"

"I'd like an ANSWER to my QUEStion! IF you can fit that into your busy SCHEDule, of course . . . I REALize that a skilled professional like yourself has many demands on her TIME. Try to fit me IN somewhere, Your Majesty! OKAY?"

Charlotte's stomach knotted, and a wave of nausea hit her; the very idea of sitting down across a table from Jerry now and eating made her feel sick. But when you have kids you have to go through the motions . . . She kept right on peeling, without a word, trying not to hear the flood of angry words, until he gave up with a curse and slammed out of the room.

There was a time when Jessica, on her way through the kitchen to her bedroom, would have stopped and asked, "Why are you crying, Mama?" But not any more. The little girl looked at Charlotte and her face fell, but she said nothing; she was learning. It broke Charlotte's heart.

✦

What's Going On Here?

Charlotte's Point of View

As Charlotte perceives it, it's despicable of her mother-in-law to call Jerry and complain about her behavior. It would be despicable even if Lydia were *right* that two bites of bacon will poison a nine-month-old child. It would be despicable if the bacon incident were *all* she told Jerry, but Charlotte is sure there was much more. Jerry knows she's careful about what she feeds the baby; if it had only been the bacon he would have come home and said, "My mother called and told me you were feeding Adam bacon this morning — do you think that's a good idea?" They would have talked about it, and she would have explained, and that would have been the end of it. Lydia must have had a lot of other things to say.

It seems to Charlotte that Jerry's behavior is equally inexcusable. In the first place, she feels that he should tell his mother to mind her own business. And if he's too cowardly to do *that*, he could at least have the decency to tell Charlotte what Lydia said and ask, courteously, for Charlotte's side of the story. *Before* he starts throwing a tantrum.

Charlotte is desperately unhappy. Trying to reason with Jerry when he's angry never helps. He loves a long, complicated debate, even though he comes out of it so wound up that it takes him hours to unwind again; and he can always out-argue her. Pleading with him doesn't help; seeing her cry only infuriates him. Fighting back is the worst of all: She always ends up apologizing to *him*, even though he started the argument, just to end the shouting match and have a little peace. And it's awful for the children when they fight. Charlotte doesn't want to live in a war zone; she hates it. But it seems to her that everything she tries to do to make it better only makes it worse, and she just doesn't know where to turn or what to do next.

Jerry's Point of View

When Lydia called Jerry about Charlotte, she had a *long* list of complaints.

Charlotte is overweight. Charlotte isn't taking care of her looks. Charlotte shouldn't wear blue jeans. Charlotte doesn't keep the kitchen clean. Charlotte is rude and stubborn and arrogant. Charlotte feeds bacon to the baby. Charlotte thinks she's important because she works in a doctor's office . . .

He'd thought his mother would never stop! He'd listened to her with half an ear, saying "Uhuh" every now and then so she'd know he was still there, trying to work on a sheet of sales figures at the same time.

"Promise me you'll *speak* to her, son!" Lydia had said, and he'd promised. Anything to shut her up. He wished she would mind her own business; he and Charlotte had a hard enough time getting along without Lydia making things worse. And he had to wonder: Did his mother really expect him to go home and tell his wife, "You're too old and too fat to wear blue jeans, and you're letting yourself go, and you don't keep the kitchen clean enough" and all the rest of that? He wouldn't have been willing to hurt Charlotte that way even if all of Lydia's accusations had been true — and they *weren't*.

But it all kept running through his mind as the day went on. It wasn't a pleasant day. He spent half of it listening to complaints from clients who didn't know what they were talking about. His new assistant crashed the computer twice, and he had to pretend he wasn't furious. The boss called a stupid meeting and he had to sit through that, biting his tongue. And he kept thinking, *Why the blazes was Charlotte so stupid as to feed the baby bacon in front of* Lydia? *Didn't she have any sense at all? Didn't she know better than to get Lydia all in a dither* (which meant Jerry would have to listen to her rant and rave)?

By the time he'd fought his way home through the traffic, he was so angry he couldn't see straight. He knew that barging in the door and yelling at Charlotte was poor strategy. On the other hand, he'd been putting up with idiots all day long. It was too much to have to deal with more of the same in his own house! And then, when Charlotte got up on her high horse and behaved as if his legitimate concern about their son's diet was beneath her lofty notice, he really lost it. Who the hell did she think she *was*?

Jerry genuinely wants peace in his home. He *needs* peace in his home. All the tension and fighting is getting to him. Everything he eats now gives him heartburn, and all he has to do to get a headache is walk in his front door. He feels completely helpless to improve matters. He's worried about the effect of all this chaos on his kids. And he knows he's not alone.

He hears it from other men, as he'd always heard it from his father: *If your house is a combat zone, if your wife has a tongue like a chainsaw and doesn't mind using it, well . . . that's* marriage *for you!* If you don't believe in knocking your wife and kids around — and Jerry most emphatically does *not* — there's nothing you can do but tough it out, they tell him. If that's true, Jerry thinks, he doesn't know how he's going to stand it.

--------------------------- ✦ ---------------------------

Both Jerry and Charlotte mean well. (For that matter, *Lydia* means well!) But they are thoroughly miserable and they've just about given up hope that their marriage will ever be anything *more* than mutual misery. They're convinced that there's nothing they can do about the polluted language environment they share. Jerry feels that Charlotte is the verbal abuser; Charlotte believes *he* is. Both feel that the other is unwilling to make even a minimal effort to keep the peace. And they and their children are paying a heavy price for this communication breakdown.

Many books (and other media) today present us with the same myth that Jerry hears from his friends and his father: the myth that if we are involved in a relationship with a verbal abuser and don't want to break it off, we're helpless to do much more than accept it and endure our misery. That's false. And there's another myth we hear all the time, the one telling us that the reason we're helpless is that you *can't* change a verbal abuser's behavior — that the change always has to be initiated *by* the abuser. That's also false. It's not hard, however, to understand where these two myths come from, and it will help if we look at three of their sources in some detail.

Myth Source One: The Idea That Verbal Abuse Is Just Like Any Other Abuse

With many other common abusive behaviors, such as alcohol or drug abuse or compulsive gambling, there really *isn't* much other people can do. It has therefore been taken for granted — incorrectly — that the same thing is true for verbal abuse.

What we overlook here is the major critical *difference* between verbal abuse and other kinds of abusive behavior, a difference so important that it cannot be overemphasized. Almost all abusive behaviors engaged in by sane human beings can be carried on alone. Most people will find it less *satisfying* to drink alone . . . or take drugs alone, or overindulge in sexual activity alone, or overwork alone . . . but all these things *can* be done alone. Verbal abuse is different; it's in a class by itself. Verbal abuse is impossible to do alone.

✦ In order to get satisfaction from verbal abuse, the abuser has to have a participating victim. It's not *like* alcohol or drugs or any of the other common abuses. In verbal abuse the "fix" (using that term very broadly) is the victim's attention and the emotional words and body language that go with it. There's no way the abuser can get that reward without a cooperating victim.

For this reason, we are *not* helpless against verbal abuse! Without our participation, it just plain isn't possible.

The verbal victim is in exactly the same situation. Without the participation of a verbal abuser, you can't *be* a verbal victim. People who are directly involved in verbal abuse can maintain that status only by functioning as verbal abuser–verbal victim *pairs;* this is a situation where it literally does "take two (or more) to tango."

Myth Source Two: Guilt

People who believe they *should* be able to change their own, or someone else's, abusive language behavior, but don't know how to go about it, are likely to feel guilty. Guilt then becomes an additional source of pain and an additional barrier to effective communication.

If You're a Verbal Victim

Verbal victims often spend a great deal of their time blaming themselves for their polluted language environment. They say, "It's all my fault" and "I must be doing something wrong or he/she wouldn't act that way" and "I must be some kind of neurotic, letting everything he/she says get to me like this."

✦   Without question, there are some verbal abusers whose behavior cannot be changed, no matter *what* the victim does, no matter *how* hard the victim tries. Such people exist; they come from that small third group described on page 39 whose verbal abuse is actually a symptom of a serious underlying problem. Faced with one of those individuals, the only alternatives may well be either to end the relationship or accept a life sentence of misery. But it's a mistake to propose that this is the *usual* situation. It's not usual; it's the exception.

For almost all verbal victims, direct or indirect, the problem is not that something is wrong with *them* but that something is wrong with their information base. They lack the information they need for using language effectively, and they are burdened with information that's inadequate or incorrect. Feeling guilty about that makes no more sense than feeling guilty because you don't know how to speak Japanese or play the cello. This information gap is something you can *fix*, and working your way through this book will take you a substantial distance toward that goal.

And what about feeling guilty because you're unable to change the language behavior of someone whose verbal abuse is a symptom?

You wouldn't feel guilty because you couldn't make your diabetic partner's pancreas produce insulin. You wouldn't say, "There must be something wrong with *me*" if your spouse had a broken leg. The situations are exactly the same. Verbal abusers who go right on with their verbal abuse even when it has no effect on their intended victims need expert help — help that can't be provided by the ordinary people around them. And they will have many other problems that make the need for such help clear. In such cases, the intended victims should feel compassion, but not guilt.

The only legitimate reason for verbal victims to feel guilty is for not *trying* . . . not trying to get the information they need, or not trying to put that information to use. It's not *like* learning Japanese or how to play the cello, where you have to start learning from scratch.

For ending verbal abuse, you already have everything you need to succeed, simply because you are a native speaker of your language. You just need a way to get at the resources you already have and begin using them in your life. And you can do that much more easily than you have been led to believe.

If You're a Verbal Abuser

Verbal abusers also frequently suffer from a terrible burden of guilt. They do know that their language is causing pain, because the evidence of that pain is clear and obvious. They're not cruel people, inflicting pain isn't their goal, and this leads to one of two consequences. Either they torment themselves because they can't keep from saying things they hate themselves for, or they escape from the torment by burying the truth about their behavior under a massive weight of *denial*.

You will know you fit the first of those descriptions if you are forever saying things like this to yourself:

"I can't believe I talked to him/her like that again . . . I must be out of my mind!"

"I swore I'd never start another fight like that again — and I did it anyway! I must be some kind of monster . . ."

"I don't know why he/she stays with me; I don't deserve it. Everybody would be a lot better off if I just went away and stayed away!"

"I can't believe I said those things to the kids . . . I could cut my tongue out! I'm not fit to have kids!"

You'll know you fit the second description, on the other hand, if you recognize your own voice in statements like these:

"It's not MY fault I keep losing my temper! If people didn't go out of their way to be irritating, it wouldn't happen!"

"I don't understand WHY he/she gets so much pleasure out of provoking me! It's STUPid!"

"If people deliberately do things that they know perfectly well I can't stand, they deserve whatever they get! It's not MY fault; I do the best I can."

"The kids know I don't mean it when I tell them I wish they'd never been born — they know I'm just tired! They're not stupid!"

"NOW look what you made me do! I hope you're PROUD of yourself!"

If you are a verbal abuser, you're right to feel guilty. The rule is simple, and we all know it well: *Causing others to feel pain is wrong.* The only exception to the rule is the situation in which something good *has* to be done and no pain-free method for accomplishing it exists — for example, giving children injections that protect them against diseases. Situations like that will come along in your life only rarely, and when they do, you'll recognize them.

However, it's one thing to feel guilt and give *up*, resulting in despair or denial. It's quite another to feel guilt and take it as a signal to change the behavior you feel guilty about. Verbal abusers are fortunate. Dependence on hurtful language is not an "addiction" like a dependence on heroin, with all of the terrible consequences of addiction. Dependence on verbal abuse, most of the time, is due to a lack of information, and that is a situation you can easily repair.

Just remember that you've had your destructive language habits for a long time. *You can't get rid of them overnight.* You've relied on them all your life long; you're likely to rely on them many more times, in spite of your good intentions. They may represent the sort of communication that you associate with your parents and relatives, people you respect and love. Change is hard; change is slow; give yourself time. If you make unreasonable demands on yourself, you risk becoming so discouraged that you lose your motivation to continue.

Giving up verbal abuse is especially difficult when you're in a close relationship with someone who has played the verbal victim role for you over a long period of time, because the temptation to maintain that familiar pattern instead of doing something new is very hard to resist. That's normal; it's part of being human. It's not a reason to feel guilty. Not as long as you keep on trying.

✦ You need to start saying, when you realize that you've been verbally abusive: "I did it again, and I feel the guilt I should feel. But failure is human. It's not a permanent condition. I've acknowledged the guilt; now I can set it aside. Instead of putting my energies into guilt, I can put them into working to do better next time."

✦ You need to start asking yourself, when you realize that you're about to say something abusive: "Why am I going to say that? What purpose does it serve for me? What's my communication goal here? What will it get me if I say that?"

With patience and persistence, you *will* be able to replace verbal abuse with language that works both for you and for the person you're talking to. This is a task you are superbly equipped to carry out.

Myth Source Three: Memories of Previous Failures

Many strategies that have been proposed for dealing with verbal abuse in a relationship actually feed the hostility and make it grow. These results have misled people, causing them to conclude that because those methods don't work, *nothing* will.

It's unfortunate that many of the methods taught for dealing with verbal abuse actually make it worse; that's not what the writers and teachers intended to have happen. The problem is that their methods are based not on contemporary linguistic science but on folklore, outdated concepts, and misconceptions. Look at the following quotation, which is the closing sentence from a story about verbal abuse in the October 12, 1992, issue of *Newsweek* magazine:

> More often than not . . . a truce will fail to hold, and the only way for
> the verbal victim to become the victor is to have the last word: good-
> bye. (Jean Seligmann et al., "The Wounds of Words," p. 92.)

This is typical; and it shows that the basic facts about verbal abuse
are still not understood. *As long as the communication goal in a relationship is to establish one person as the "victor" (winner) and the
other as the loser, no positive change is ever going to be possible.*
This crucial misunderstanding of the facts makes the best-intentioned
attempts to teach techniques for change useless, and the result is a
series of failures which support the myth that nothing can be done.

Suppose you are the victim in a verbally abusive relationship,
and you're determined to try to fix that. You read a book (or take a
course, or attend a seminar) that will allegedly provide you with
tools for ending the abuse. You invest your resources — your time,
your money, your energy — in the techniques you learn. You do your
very best; you try *hard*. AND IT DOESN'T WORK. Either nothing
changes, or the only change is a change for the worse.

At that point, your tendency is to conclude that all the people
who've been telling you nothing can be done were right, and that
you were foolish to doubt them. This is natural. After all — you
believed the experts, you did what they told you to do, to the best of
your ability, and it was all for nothing.

You know, from reading *this* book, that countering verbal abuse
with more verbal abuse, or with logical arguments, or with pleading,
only feeds the habit and makes it grow. What most systems for handling verbal abuse teach is how to counterattack or debate or plead
more effectively. The very techniques they teach are techniques for
feeding the verbal violence loop more assertively. More *skill*fully.
THIS ISN'T GOING TO WORK. All the good intentions in the
world, all the hard work in the world, won't make it work, because:

◆ IF YOU ALWAYS SAY THE WRONG THING, LEARNING
    TO SAY IT MORE ELOQUENTLY AND EFFECTIVELY
    WON'T HELP.

What you need (and what this eight-step program provides) is
effective language patterns to replace the ones that don't work. It's
just that simple.

The Grammar of Verbal Violence

At this point you may have some compelling questions. For example:

1. *Why should you believe* me*?*

2. *What is there about the techniques this book teaches that makes them any more effective than the ones I've said can't possibly work?*

3. *So my techniques are based on contemporary linguistic science — so what? What difference does that make to you?*

4. *So other experts have good intentions but are mistaken — what reason do you have to think that isn't also true of me?*

These are excellent questions. You *should* ask them. You have every right to know the answers.

I can tell you first of all that the *Gentle Art of Verbal Self-Defense* system on which this program is based has been tested all over this country, in every sort of real-world situation, by every sort of person, for more than two decades. I know, from the volume of letters and calls and reports I receive, that the system works. That's important.

But what's more important, and what gives me the confidence to make the claims I do, is the fact that the system I teach relies on *your* strengths, not mine or those of other experts and scholars and scientists. Its foundation is the flawless internal grammar of your language, which has been yours since childhood and is as much a part of you as your eyes and your heart.

Go to an elementary school playground some day and spend half an hour listening to small children who aren't getting along together. Listen to the things they say. You'll find that they don't have as sophisticated a vocabulary as adult speakers do. You'll find that they aren't as inhibited about expressing their feelings as adult speakers are; they're a lot less worried about seeming rude . . . or crude . . . than most grownups. But you will hear them using exactly the same *patterns* of verbal abuse that adults use. They already know how, and their competence in putting those patterns to use will only improve as the children grow older and get more practice.

In the next chapter of this book we'll discuss the concept of the internal grammar in detail. For now, I just want to point out that the grammar of verbal violence is *included* in every English speaker's internal grammar. When you use English to convey an insult, a threat, ridicule, sarcasm, or a verbal attack, you use that internal grammar. When you are in the verbal victim role and you use English to plead with a verbal abuser or to debate one, you use that grammar. And it is the resource that involved bystanders rely on in order to recognize and understand the verbal abuse going on around them.

Your long-term memory contains a perfect grammar of English, and of English verbal violence. *You know all about it.* A grammar is nothing more than a set of rules. *You know them all.* A system based on *that* foundation is as reliable as gravity, and you can count on it.

What to Do about It:
Choosing Your Communication Strategy

The idea in the *Newsweek* quotation on page 66 is not just a careless comment. It represents a communication strategy in which the goal of the verbal victim is to become the *winner* in language interactions with the verbal abuser. The existence of a winner presupposes that there is also a loser; the strategy is also, therefore, to make the verbal abuser lose. This is a change, certainly. But it's a change that does nothing but switch the power rankings. The relationship itself does not change: It continues to revolve around linguistic *combat*.

Most of us are not accustomed to the idea that we should go into communication with a clear strategy, carefully chosen and planned to achieve specific communication goals. We plan the *action* we're going to take . . . we plan to present a proposal, or demand a raise, or argue about a grade, or complain about a late delivery . . . but we don't plan the language strategy we'll use to carry out that action. This is a mistake, because the choice of strategy in many ways determines what sort of language behavior must be used to achieve the goal.

Suppose you are obliged to spend a substantial amount of time with someone who consistently talks to you in a disrespectful manner; let's call this person "Tracy" to simplify matters. Suppose

Tracy's behavior distresses you and you intend to go to Tracy and make that clear. A number of communication strategies are then available to you, each with its own best language choices. Here are the most obvious ones:

1. To get your anger at Tracy off your chest.

2. To become the winner in your encounters with Tracy and make Tracy the loser.

3. To educate Tracy about the error of his or her ways.

4. To persuade Tracy to stop talking to you disrespectfully.

If your goal is just to vent your anger, you can achieve it by almost any sort of hostile language you care to use. If your goal is to be the winner in a winner-loser relationship, your strategy will be to come up with counterattacks or logical arguments that Tracy won't be able to top. If educating Tracy is your goal, you'll want to prepare for a lecture or sermon. However, if your goal is to persuade Tracy to stop using disrespectful language toward you, you will need something else. There are major advantages to persuading, as opposed to forcing. People who are *forced* to do something differently will resent that and look for ways to get revenge, or will shift their negative behavior to some other victim, or both.

Before you talk to Tracy, you need to decide which of these goals is the one that matters most to you, because each requires different language behavior and you can't do more than one of them at a time.

The best technique I know for persuading someone to honor a complaint is the construction of a sequence called a *three-part message*. Let's look at this technique.

Using the Three-Part Message

You may have heard of something called an "I-message," in which the complainer is supposed to clearly state his or her feelings about a specific behavior. For example, "I feel angry when you forget to water the tomato plants." An I-message is definitely an improvement over the vague or judgmental complaints many of us make. But there is a better way. Dr. Thomas Gordon, the effectiveness training expert, developed the I-message further by adding a third section to the pattern, like this:

> "When you forget to water the tomato plants, I feel angry, because they die without water."

The three-part message begins by stating the specific item of behavior you want changed, goes on to state the emotion you feel about that behavior, and ends by stating the real-world consequences of the behavior that justify the complaint. Putting the "when" chunk first is good strategy, because it emphasizes the *behavior* rather than the emotion. Ideally, as in the example just given, none of the three parts contains anything that can reasonably be argued about. This is enormously better than the typical way of handling the situation, as in these examples:

> "You PROMised me you'd WATER the toMAtoes, and you for-GOT! I can't trust you to do ANYthing right!"

> "How could you POSSIBLY forget to water the toMAtoes? Don't you have any sense at ALL?"

> "If you had any sense at ALL, you would reMEMber to water the toMAtoes!"

> "Don't you EVer forget to water the tomatoes again! I won't STAND for it!"

> "PLEASE don't forget to water the tomatoes! They'll DIE if you don't take care of them! I can't do EVERYthing around here!"

> "Reliable people live up to their obligations—when they're supposed to water plants, they can be counted on to do it. It would be advisable to try to meet that standard in the future."

All of these utterances have their purposes and will achieve a goal. But *none* of them is likely to persuade the other person to change the behavior being objected to. Adults in our society resent being told what to do — even indirectly — by other adults, and that resentment is a sturdy barrier against change. Using the three-part message is a far better strategy.

Another Look at Scenario Three

Scenario Three shows us another unpleasant scene between Jerry and Charlotte Brown. We know they care about each other and about their marriage, but the language they use in the scenario seems as tailored to *destroy* their relationship as possible. They're not using their fists, but they're causing each other pain that is just as dangerous as physical blows. And they're both convinced that they're doing everything that *can* be done to make things better. Let's analyze one of their exchanges — an attack and a response — to see what's going on and find out how it could be improved.

Jerry: "Dammit, Charlotte! What's the MATTER with you, ANYway, giving Adam BACon? You're supposed to KNOW something about feeding kids, RIGHT? Listen — EVen JESSica would know better than to load a baby up with SALT and FAT!"

Charlotte: [A tight-lipped, silent stare.]

Remember that this utterance of Jerry's (which is a single connected chunk of speech, one conversational turn) is the *first one* in the conversation, spoken the instant he was inside the door. He didn't even say "Hello" before he lashed into his tirade. Forget the words he uses for a moment, and consider only the tune he's set them to: Anyone hearing him would know he was furious, even if they were too far *away* to understand the words.

We can imagine situations in which such speech would be appropriate. For example:

Jerry: "Dammit, Charlotte! What's the MATTER with you, ANYway, striking a match to check for a GAS leak? YOU'LL blow up the whole HOUSE!"

But the situation in the scenario is not an emergency, and the way Jerry is saying those words is *not* appropriate. However . . . he can't help being angry. He had a frustrating day filled with unpleasant situations he was powerless to change, including an unpleasant interaction with his interfering mother. Choking back the anger — which *is* what he does in his relationship with Lydia — could have only two consequences: Either he would add to the burden of suppressed tension and stress that is already causing him health problems, or he would unload the suppressed anger on someone other than Charlotte . . . one of the children, for example. What Jerry needs is something he can say that releases some of his tension without wreaking havoc. For example:

> "Hello, Charlotte. I want to warn you — I've had one hell of a day and I'm so damned mad I don't trust myself to talk. I'm going upstairs for a few minutes; I'll be down as soon as I stop feeling like Attila the Hun."

Followed by a swift exit up the stairs, and time alone, while he calms down.

✦ WARNING: Charlotte can ruin this, easily. All she has to do is follow Jerry up the stairs, demanding that he tell her what's wrong, right now. Or, when he comes back down, she can greet him with any one of these:

• "WELL? Are you ready to TALK NOW?"

• "That was a disgusting performance, Jerry; I hope the second act is better than the first one."

• "Listen — I do NOT intend to put up with the kind of theatrics you just laid on here. Don't EVer do that again."

• "Jerry, I don't know WHY you were so angry . . . but I'm REALLY SORRy! Whatever it was I did — PLEASE forgive me?"

• [A tight-lipped, silent stare.]

If she avoids those moves and greets him neutrally, ready to listen, *he will say what she thought he ought to say.* That is, he will say, "Honey, my mother called me today and said that you've been feeding Adam bacon. Do you think that's a good idea?" To which she can answer, "I feed him a piece of bacon about one inch square, Jerry, and I do it maybe once a month. I'm afraid I wasn't able to make Lydia understand that." To which he can say, "I figured that was all it was, but I had so much stupid stuff to put up with today that I let it get to me. Sorry." And they can eat their dinner in peace.

If Jerry *doesn't* change his opening utterance, Charlotte is justified in feeling abused. And she has a choice of strategies. She can use that justification as a reason to feed the verbal violence loop Jerry started, knowing that he is in the wrong and she is in the right. Making that choice will end with her crying at the sink as she peels the potatoes, with Jessica frightened again and another evening ruined — but it's her privilege, and Jerry knew that when he started the row.

Let's consider this choice — being right, and damn the consequences — as if it were part of a football game:

✦ It's the right strategy if your goal is to win on one play. It's the *wrong* strategy if your goal is to win the *game.*

The choice that wins the game . . . the choice that means an evening of pleasant companionship for a change and sets a precedent for more such evenings . . . is this one:

Jerry: "Dammit, Charlotte, what's the MATTER with you . . . " *(And all the rest of the tirade, as before.)*

Charlotte: "Jerry, I know you too well to believe you'd be this angry over one little piece of bacon. You must have spent the whole day in a pressure cooker, including a long conversation with your mother about my many failings. Want to start over and tell me about it?"

For Charlotte to answer this way doesn't allow her the pleasure that comes with a feeling of righteous outrage and moral superiority. It doesn't allow her the pleasure that comes from being "the winner." It *does* allow her the pleasure that comes from demonstrating her skill at effective communication. It doesn't require her to sacrifice her dignity or her principles. It doesn't require her to plead, debate, or counterattack. And unlike the sequence of events in the scenario, it can't be interpreted as an attempt to *punish* Jerry, raise his consciousness, or make him feel guilty. It says, "I see and hear and feel your anger; I know it's real. I'm willing to discuss it if you are."

There isn't room in this book to take up each pair of utterances in the scenario and analyze them with revisions and comments. That's unfortunate, because just *one* such exchange may not be enough. It may take two or three. (You might try doing this yourself; it would be a useful exercise.) But the principles would be the same in every case, for each pair — and you have the rules of your grammar, which don't have to fit between the covers of a book, to fall back on. In every case, Jerry and Charlotte should stop before speaking and ask themselves these two questions:

1. What am I trying to accomplish with what I'm going to say?

2. Is there another way to accomplish the same goal, without feeding the verbal violence loop and without sacrificing my dignity?

This would be a new way of communicating, for both Jerry and Charlotte. At first it would be hard for them to remember to do it, and it would seem awkward and difficult and contrived, just as it's awkward and difficult and contrived at first to go down a hill on skis when you've always *walked* down before. But it's something they certainly can do, if they're willing to make the effort; and the results are sure to be a major improvement. After a while it would stop being new and awkward and become as automatic as the confrontations and scenes that have for so long been their customary way of handling conflict.

Step 3 Backup

Verbal Abuse Incident Log

This diary page is designed to let you accomplish three useful tasks:

1. To track your own involvement in verbal abuse.

2. To become consciously aware of your personal language strategies in verbal confrontations and disagreements.

3. To determine what the *consequences* of your language strategies are.

Under "Description of the Language" write down as accurately as you can what the other person(s) involved in the incident said, what you said back, and so on—as if you were writing the dialogue for a play. Describe the body language that went with the words, too: tone of voice, facial expression, gestures, and posture. Don't worry about being unable to remember every detail; that's to be expected. Just record as much information as you can.

DATE: _____

DESCRIPTION OF THE SITUATION:

MY ROLE:

(I was the abuser/the victim/the involved bystander.)

DESCRIPTION OF THE LANGUAGE:

(Who said what, to whom, and in what way.)

75

ANALYSIS

1. What were my feelings—the *emotion(s)* that I felt—during this interaction?

2. What were my physical reactions during this interaction? (Examples: My head started hurting . . . The palms of my hands got sweaty . . . My heart started pounding and my chest felt tight.)

3. What were my feelings and my physical reactions when the interaction was over?

4. What were the *consequences* of the incident? (Examples: It spoiled the holiday for everybody who was there . . . She started crying, and I felt terrible about it . . . I completely forgot what I was supposed to be doing, and then my boss was furious with me the next morning.)

5. If I could do the whole thing over again, how would I handle it? What would I do differently?

TOTAL NUMBER OF VERBAL ABUSE INCIDENTS I'VE BEEN INVOLVED IN SO FAR THIS MONTH:

As a verbal abuser _____

As a verbal victim _____

As an involved bystander _____

Three-Part Message Log

The goal of this diary page is to help you learn to use the three-part message patterns with ease and skill when you need to make a complaint or request a change in someone else's behavior. Remember the example of a perfect three-part message: "When you don't water the tomato plants, I feel angry, because plants die when they don't get watered."

DATE: _____

DESCRIPTION OF THE SITUATION

THE SPECIFIC ITEM OF BEHAVIOR THAT I WANTED CHANGED:

THE THREE-PART MESSAGE THAT I USED:

WHAT THE OTHER PERSON SAID IN REPLY:

WHAT HAPPENED—THE CONSEQUENCES:

(Examples: He never did that again . . . He kept right on "forgetting" to do the dishes, but he started apologizing for forgetting; that's progress! . . . It didn't stop the behavior, but now it happens only once a month instead of every two or three days . . . She was stunned—she'd had no idea I minded; and she promised not to do it again.)

(And if things did not go well . . .)

WHAT WENT WRONG:

HOW I COULD HAVE MADE MY THREE-PART MESSAGE BETTER:

COMMENTS:

Communication Strategy Log

This diary page will help you begin actively using communication strategies, and will let you observe your progress over time. (If you have more than one communication goal in a single situation, it's best to use a separate page for each goal.)

DATE: _____

DESCRIPTION OF THE SITUATION:

MY COMMUNICATION GOAL WAS:

(Examples: To make my kids understand that I really need some peace and quiet when I first get up in the morning . . . To help my boss understand why we can't possibly finish all the work that comes in on Friday before the weekend . . . To change my friend's attitude about watching football games.)

THE COMMUNICATION STRATEGY I CHOSE FOR WORKING TOWARD THAT GOAL:

(Examples: I decided to use a three-part message . . . I waited until we were alone, and then I explained, being very careful to sound as neutral as possible.)

WHAT HAPPENED—THE CONSEQUENCES:

(And if things did not go well . . .)

WHAT I SHOULD HAVE DONE INSTEAD:

COMMENTS:

Letters You Don't Send

One of the oldest and most reliable ways to deal with the need to just get your emotions off your chest (and out of your head) without negative consequences is to *write a letter that you don't send.* Write it to the person you're angry with, or to someone you're tempted to talk to about your anger. Write down everything you want so badly to *say* to that person; write it *instead* of saying it. Get it all out of your system.

And then: DON'T SEND THE LETTER. The best thing to do is destroy it, so that you can be sure no one but you will ever see it. But if you feel that you need to keep it awhile—perhaps so you can read it again in a week or two to find out whether you would still feel the emotion as strongly as you did when you wrote it—keep it strictly to yourself. You'll only feel free to write frankly if you know that you are your only audience.

You may think that this couldn't possibly be of any use. After all, the circumstances that you reacted to with the unpleasant emotion haven't changed in any way; everything is still just as it was. But there's something tremendously helpful about moving all that negative language *out*, where you can look at it as an object—as something that you can revise or erase or tear into pieces or anything else you might choose to do *to* a letter. One of the major causes of misery is the feeling of having no *control* over the things that cause you pain; and when we have a sort of "tape" playing in our head, composed of all the things we *want* to say, we often feel that we can't stop it from playing over and over again. That's an illusion, but it *feels* real, and it can be a torment. Writing the letter you don't send will STOP THE TAPE, giving you back the knowledge that you *do* have control.

✦ SIGHT BITES ✦
Quotations to Think About and Use

"Look upon him who shows you your faults as a revealer of treasure . . ."

(The *Dhammapada*, verse 76.)

"People are frequently fatalistic about their ways of communicating. They tend to think that their way of talking and listening, like the color of their eyes, is a 'given' in their lives. To try to change one's style of communication, so the argument goes, is impossible. . . . My experience and that of my colleagues in teaching communication skills to thousands of people leads to just the opposite conclusion."

(Bolton 1987, p. 10.)

"When Archie Bunker called Edith a dingbat and admonished her, 'Stifle yourself,' we laughed. But in real life verbal abuse is anything but funny. It can warn of physical abuse to come — and even all by itself can destroy a relationship."

(Seligman et al. 1992, p. 90.)

"A speaker . . . has to solve the problem: 'Given that I want to bring about such-and-such a result in the hearer's consciousness, what is the best way to accomplish this aim by using language?'"

(G. Leech, quoted in Renkema 1993, p. x.)

◆

Recognizing That You Are an Expert in Your Language

*I know that I am an expert in my language
and superbly skilled in its use. I know that my
grammar is as much a part of me as my lungs
and my heart; I will not allow the mythologies of
grades and test scores to lessen my respect for my
internal grammar.*

Scenario Four

"Jessica Brown, you're not doing your <u>work</u>! <u>Again</u>! Why <u>not</u>?" Jessica sat, trying not to squirm — Mr. Lopez really got mad if you didn't sit still when he was talking to you! — and hoping her face didn't show what she was thinking.

"Well, Jessica?" he demanded. "What do you have to <u>say</u> for yourself?"

She swallowed hard, while he drummed impatiently on the edge of her desk with one finger, and she managed to choke out, "I don't <u>get</u> it, <u>that's</u> all!"

"Jessica, your only problem is that you won't <u>try</u>. Look at the <u>page</u>, Jessica! Everything you need to know is <u>right there</u>, right before your eyes, if you'll just <u>look</u> at it!"

"Okay, Mr. Lopez!"

"We do <u>not</u> say 'okay' to our teacher!" he snapped, and Jessica

81

nodded her head as fast as she could, saying "I mean <u>Yes</u>, Mr. Lopez!"

"The information isn't written in your <u>lap</u>, Jessica!" said the teacher, sounding as if he'd had all he could stand and then some, and Jessica felt her cheeks turn bright red . . . she could hear the other kids giggling.

"<u>Well</u>, Jessica?"

What does he want me to say? the child thought, panicked. *I don't know what to <u>say</u>!* And she blurted out again, "Mr. Lopez, I just don't <u>get</u> it! I can't <u>do</u> it—it's too <u>hard</u>!"

He stood there, staring at her in silence, his arms folded over his chest, shaking his head; and then he sighed heavily. "Very well, Jessica," he said. "If you refuse to do your grammar page, you'll just have to accept the consequences. We'll see what your <u>parents</u> have to say about it, young lady!"

And then he turned his back on her and went to his desk and sat down, without giving her a chance to say another word.

I never said I wouldn't do my page! Jessica thought angrily, *I never <u>said</u> that! He's just <u>mean</u>!*

When Jessica got home that afternoon, she handed her mother the note from Mr. Lopez and waited anxiously, biting her lip.

But all Charlotte said was, "Hmmmmmmmmmm." That didn't tell Jessica much.

"Are you mad at me, Mama?"

"No, Jessie, I'm not mad at you."

"Can I . . . Is it okay to ask you what it says?"

"It says you make silly excuses to get out of doing the grammar pages in your workbook, honey."

"But, Mama, I—"

Charlotte touched the child's lips gently with one finger, hushing her. "It's all right," she said, thinking what a rotten teacher young John Lopez was, and wishing she could tell Jessica *that*. "Don't worry about it, honey. I always hated grammar, too, and I never did very well in it. It's no big deal. Just do the best you can."

"Okay, Mama," Jessica answered dubiously. "But I don't <u>get</u> it," she added. It was true. She really *didn't*. She didn't understand one single word Mr. Lopez said when he talked about those pages.

Charlotte gave her a quick hug. "Never mind," she said. "Go play, and then when you come in you can set the table for me."

Charlotte watched Jessica go out the door, and then she read the note again, her lips tight. She could tell Jessica it wasn't important; that was her honest opinion. But she had to think of something more diplomatic to say to John Lopez, or she'd end up sitting through one of his parent-teacher conference lectures . . . horrible thought. "The parent must instill the proper values in the child!" he would say. Pompous, that's what he was. Pompous and pedantic. Maybe next year Jessica would get a teacher with a little more experience . . . she hoped so.

Charlotte agreed with Mr. Lopez that teaching a child the importance of education was properly the parents' job. But if the teacher teaches the child to hate school, what are the parents supposed to do? *Poor Adam!*, she thought sadly, hearing the baby fussing in his crib, *I'm glad you don't know what's ahead of you!*

-------------------------- ✦ --------------------------

What's Going On Here?

John Lopez's Point of View

As John Lopez perceives it, Jessica Brown is one of the luckiest kids in his class. Both of her parents are professionals with steady jobs and decent paychecks; she has a nice home and pretty clothes; her mother is almost always there when she gets home; she has a fancy lunch packed every day in a handsome bright lunchbox, and money to spend on Book Fair days. Jessica has it easy, and he is sure her parents spoil her. Seeing her sit, sullen and squirming, looking out the window and up at the ceiling and down at her lap, *anywhere* but at her work or her teacher, makes him so mad he can't see straight. He tries to be fair with Jessica, but she's difficult to talk to — all he has to do is say two words and she starts cowering and turning first red and then white, as if he were some kind of brute that eats little kids for breakfast. It baffles him. He's never struck a child in his life, and he never would; he tries very hard to be a *good* teacher. Nothing else matters to him as much as his students do; they come first, always. What, he wonders, is *wrong* with Jessica Mary Brown, *any*way?

Jessica's Point of View

For Jessica, the problem is that she has trouble understanding as fast as the other kids in the class, and she keeps falling behind. The things the teacher says about the workbook pages don't make much sense to her, especially since she *knows* she's not going to be able to do them right. When she tries to get Mr. Lopez to help her catch up, she can't think of any way to word her questions, and that makes her so flustered that pretty soon she can't think of anything to say at *all*. She knows she rubs her teacher the wrong way, and she does everything she can to stay out of trouble. And she works *hard* to keep up. Jessica can think of nothing worse in all the world than the possibility that she might get kept back and have to do second grade with Mr. Lopez over again!

Charlotte's Point of View

Charlotte knows what it's like to have a teacher make you feel so stupid and scared that you can't talk; she's had teachers like that herself, as has everyone. If Mr. Lopez called Jessica names or threatened her or was openly abusive, she would go talk to him about it, but she knows he's not like that. He's just young and inexperienced and has no idea how deeply his words can cut a child. Charlotte wishes there were a way to teach Jessica — and Adam — how to defend themselves, how to stand up to unfair teachers without getting into trouble, how to make their needs *clear* with their words . . . but everyone knows this is just something children have to pick up as they go along. That's the way life is; it's not fair, but there's nothing you can do most of the time except hang in there.

———————————————— ✦ ————————————————

These are typical ideas and attitudes, with which many people would readily agree. They would be mistaken in doing so. Because the things that John Lopez and Charlotte and Jessica "know" in this situation are for the most part false.

Every one of us, like Charlotte and Jessica, has had at least one teacher whose class we dreaded, whose words and manner made us feel like crawling into a hole and pulling it in after us. And almost every one of us has taken at least one class where we got lost at the beginning and kept right on being lost all the way to the end. We've all had the experience of understanding so little of a subject that we couldn't figure out how to word our questions. We would all agree with Charlotte — it's not fair, but that's the way life is.

However, it's truly astonishing that we experience this kind of confusion and distress in classes that are about our native *language!* If any subject should be easy and enjoyable for us, it's "language arts" classes in our native tongue. Instead, most people remember such courses with guarded tolerance; far too many remember them with loathing. This is a sad state of affairs. It has made us a nation of people who excuse their communication problems by claiming, like Charlotte Brown, that they've "never been any good at grammar." It is the result of a lack of valid information about how human languages are learned and used.

You Are an Expert in Your Language

Our knowledge of our language is different from our knowledge of math and science and history. Like knowing how to walk upright, it's part of the unique kind of knowledge called *internalized* knowledge. When we use internalized information we can do it almost automatically, without even having to think about it, without having to work at remembering it, without being able to explain what we're doing. People can take a religious vow of silence, or go to live in a foreign country, and speak their language rarely or not at all for many years. Nevertheless, although when they try to speak it again they may be a bit awkward at first, they won't have forgotten it. Unlike other subjects we study, language is in many ways independent of intelligence; only in very *severe* mental retardation do we find children who are exposed to human language in infancy failing to learn to speak that language.

By the time we start school we have an essentially complete mastery of the grammar of our language. By age five or so we can ask questions and understand answers, give orders, make statements and promises and threats, and carry on a sensible conversation. We may still say "wabbit" for "rabbit." We don't have an adult vocabulary. And we lack experience with *pragmatics* (the intersection of language and the real world), where we have to know such things as when it is or isn't appropriate to tell a joke. Our grasp of conversational strategies is very limited, but we know the basic grammar — the patterns for forming our words and sentences correctly — almost completely. We don't go into the study of any other subject with a knowledge base even remotely like that. Let's take just a minute to look at an example that will make the process easier to understand.

One Kapooz, Many Kapoozes

Suppose you show some five-year-olds a picture of an imaginary creature and say, "Kids, this is a wappler." Then you show them a picture of *two* of the creatures and ask, "And these are some . . . whats?" The children will immediately answer, "Wapplers!" and they will pronounce the "s" at the end as if it were a "z." If you show them a picture of one creature you call a "blappit," and then a picture of several, they'll identify the second picture as more "blappits" and pronounce the "s" *as* "s" that time. Finally, shown a picture of one "kapooz," they'll call three of them "kapoozes," correctly adding the "uh" between "z" and "s" and pronouncing the final "s" as "z."

◆ This is an extraordinarily complex performance, based on very sophisticated information, and it happens at a time when these children don't even know the *names* of "s" and "z" yet. It clearly demonstrates why it's possible for us to grow up believing that good language skills are possible only for the brilliant, the lucky, and people with Ph.D.s in English. Our problem is that we don't *know* what we know.

Five-year-olds can't tell you that the rule for forming plurals is "Add an 's' at the end of the word." They can't tell you that the plural ending "s" is pronounced three different ways, depending on what class of sounds the final sound in the word comes from. They can't explain that the reason for the "uh" in "kapoozes" is that English doesn't allow any word to contain an "s" followed by a "z." But the fact that they *use* those rules with ease proves that they *do know* them, as do you. You demonstrate your mastery of the system for using your language hundreds of times a day by speaking, just as you demonstrate your mastery of the system for using a car by driving. Being able (or unable) to recite the rules has nothing at all to do with it.

Unfortunately, when children are five or six years old, we send them to school to study the grammar they already know and we start giving them grades on their performance. This book is not the place to argue about how our educational system handles such matters. The results, however, are obvious and beyond argument: A large percentage of our population comes out of the final years of school convinced — incorrectly — that they are only just barely competent in their language.

We don't learn that we have a flawless internal grammar that we can always rely on and for which we should have great respect. No one ever tells us that. We certainly don't suspect that we were already experts before we *started* studying "grammar."

It's hard to convince adults who've always felt defensive about their "language arts skills" of these facts, but it's important to do so. We adults need to realize that we are *still* experts in our language. Whether our confidence in our mastery of our native tongue has been destroyed as we were growing up or not, we still know all the things we knew at five. In addition, we know all the things we've learned since, such as the words in our much larger adult vocabularies, which parts of our native dialects are likely to annoy purists, and a multitude of facts about what mainstraim English speakers consider to be correct *usage*.

✦ The internalized knowledge we have of our language can be taken away from us only by medical catastrophes. However, our lack of information and confidence about that knowledge can keep us from making full use of it.

The information in our internal grammars goes far beyond rules about making plurals and shaping questions. Our mental grammar tells us whether a sequence of language is a promise or a threat or a joke or a marriage proposal. It tells us whether it is or isn't appropriate to respond by laughing, or shaking our head, or making an angry remark. It tells us how close to another person from our own culture we should stand when we talk. It tells us how *fast* we should talk, and how loud. It tells us whether we're involved in a conversation or an interview or a formal interrogation. It can't tell us exactly what words will be said back to us when we speak, but it does tell us whether the response we hear is or isn't appropriate. Finally, included in that wonderful grammar is the English grammar of verbal abuse and verbal violence, *in which we are also experts.*

There are two reasons why this information is crucially important to putting an end to verbal abuse in our lives.

1. If we are to take control of our language environment, we have to get past the mythology that causes otherwise capable and competent adults to say things like, "My grammar really isn't very good — I never got better than C's in English." We have to learn to respect and trust our internal grammars, because failing to do so keeps us from making maximum use of our language skills.

2. Knowing the truth about our internal grammars helps us understand that verbal abuse is almost never an innocent mistake. If we are verbal abusers, we cannot truthfully say we didn't know our words would hurt the persons we said them to. We *do* know, because that knowledge is stored in our internal grammar.

When verbal abusers try to excuse their language behavior with "But I didn't mean to hurt your feelings," it's usually the truth, in the sense that their goal was not to cause pain. But when their excuse is that they didn't *know* the words would hurt ("But all I *said* was . . ."), they're not being truthful. *They know better.* Once in a great while, verbal abuse is an accident, but only once in a great while. Most of the time, although the primary purpose for the abusive language is to get attention and demonstrate power, verbal abusers are entirely aware that it will cause pain and resentment and distress. That's why they chose it. They know language that hurts is more likely to get attention and provoke an emotional reaction than language that doesn't.

What to Do about It: Giving Up the Myths about Verbal Abuse

If You're a Verbal Abuser

Myth: "Hey, I didn't <u>mean</u> to hurt your feelings!"

Myth: "Only <u>wimps</u> get their feelings hurt!"

As long as we can convince ourselves that we didn't know our words were going to cause pain . . . as long as we can convince ourselves that we're innocent, and that people who take offense at our words are neurotic or foolish . . . as long as we can maintain those illusions, we're unlikely to be able to give up the verbal violence habit. And verbal victims who accept our phony excuses — like "I had no <u>idea</u> that you'd mind if I said that!" and "All I <u>said</u> was . . ." and "Hey, can't you take a <u>joke</u>?" — aren't helping us. They're making it easier for us to go on believing the myths, and they're training us to be ever better verbal abusers, with guaranteed negative consequences down the road.

If You're a Verbal Victim

Myth: "I'm just not any <u>good</u> at language — I never <u>have</u> been!"

Myth: "But there's nothing I can do . . . I can't just be <u>rude</u> to people!"

Similarly, if we are verbal victims we also have to give up some myths. It's false, and an insult to our magnificent human brains, to insist that we "aren't good enough with language" to establish a language environment around us that is usually free of verbal violence.

There's no law that says we have to respond to verbal abuse with more abuse, or logical arguments, or pathetic pleas. We have to give up the myth that we're helpless and stop *participating* in episodes of verbal violence. We have to set aside the myths that we're being "nice" or kind when we accept the verbal abuser's phony excuses. We are fully capable of doing all these things.

If You're an Involved Bystander

Myth: "But I can't just leave! I can't just walk out!"

Unless we are literally in danger from the people carrying on verbal abuse in our presence, we have to give up the myth that we are obligated to *stay* while they do it. It's perfectly appropriate to leave the scene of verbal violence and refuse to be a passive participant.

The Most Dangerous Myth of All

Above all, verbal abusers, verbal victims, and involved bystanders have to give up the "Sticks and stones will break my bones, but *words* will never hurt me!" myth. Our society can no longer afford the luxury of letting that one survive.

Verbal abuse is as dangerous as a speeding truck to both victims *and* abusers, and only slightly less dangerous to involved bystanders. The damage doesn't happen as fast and isn't as easy to see, but it's just as serious. Verbal abuse is the major factor behind the chronic hostility and loneliness that contributes so substantially to our illnesses and injuries. It destroys marriages, interferes with our parenting, and turns our workplaces into prisons. It's ruining our health care and justice systems, and making a mockery of our systems of education. It is the root of the epidemic of *physical* violence we suffer from today. At every turn, verbal abuse has negative consequences in our lives.

We have to become aware that we *don't* have to put up with this situation. We are fully equipped — with our flawless internal grammars and our reliable common sense — to use language in ways that defuse hostility and put an end to verbal abuse.

If it were true that we couldn't do anything about verbal violence, it would be tragic. Verbal abuse would then be a natural disaster, like earthquakes and tornadoes are. Equipped as we are to stop it, however, letting verbal abuse ruin our lives is worse than tragic. Toxic language is one kind of pollution that we do *not* have to tolerate.

Another Look at Scenario Four

This scenario shows us two typical examples of the cultural processes that cause children to grow up into adults who can't deal with verbal abuse effectively.

Jessica and Her Teacher

First, we see a seven-year-old girl being verbally bullied by someone who outranks her in every way: He's an adult, he's male, and he's her teacher. He pins her down in front of her classmates and demands, repeatedly, that she explain why she isn't doing the workbook page he assigned.

Jessica's panic in this situation would make it hard for her to talk even if she knew what she wanted to say. Since she is so confused that she can't even form a sensible question, she has no chance at all. And it's clear that this is a pattern that goes on between John Lopez and Jessica all the time — it's a *chronic* problem. Some children in a situation like this one rebel vigorously and become "bad" kids; others, like Jessica, become verbal victims. The victim role comes easily to Jessica because it is the role her mother models for her at home. *This is where it starts — in childhood.*

Jessica and Her Mother

Second, we see Charlotte failing to offer Jessica any help at all in dealing with the teacher. Charlotte clearly knows what's going on; she remembers facing the same dilemma when she was a schoolchild. She is sympathetic, and she offers Jessica comfort and reassurance.

But the only *strategy* she proposes to her daughter is that of sweeping the whole problem under the rug. "Don't worry about it," she tells the child. "I always hated grammar, too, and I never did very well in it. It's no big deal."

Charlotte fails Jessica here. Not because she's an uncaring mother; not because she doesn't want to bother helping. Charlotte grew up like most of us do, unaware of her own linguistic potential, accepting the idea that only "experts" have really good language skills and that everybody else has to just muddle along as best they can. She is building that same conviction in Jessica, destructive as it is to the child's ability to *use* her language, because she honestly believes that it's valid. Again — this is where it starts.

There's a Better Way

Suppose that it were different; suppose John Lopez and Jessica Brown were both able to use language effectively. How would their dialogue have been different?

Teacher: "Jessica, you're not doing the workbook page. Can you tell me why?"

Jessica: "I just don't get it, Mr. Lopez."

Teacher: "You don't understand the page?"

Jessica: "No, sir. I don't understand at <u>all</u>. I don't know how to do it."

After which Mr. Lopez could have sat down with Jessica and helped her then and there, or had her come to his desk for help, or asked her to stay in at recess (or after school) for help, or asked another pupil to work with her . . . any one of a number of helping behaviors, depending on the time he has available and his teaching style.

Unfortunately, he doesn't know how to question an anxious child without turning it into an *interrogation,* and the panic he sees in Jessica only makes him more punitive. *He* knows he doesn't mean to frighten her, and he can certainly see that she doesn't understand that. But instead of recognizing her lack of comprehension as his own failure to make his meaning clear, plus her lack of skill at adult-child conversation, he leaps to conclusions about her *character.* She isn't trying; she's disrespectful; her parents spoil her; she's making silly excuses to get out of doing her work.

✦ This is the standard pattern: Instead of recognizing that the problem is the language, he assumes that the problem is the person.

Alternatively, what if the interaction at school went on as shown in the scenario, but Charlotte knew how to be more helpful? Let's look at how the dialogue might have gone, starting where (in the original version) Charlotte tells Jessica not to worry about it.

Charlotte: "Honey, can you tell me exactly what happened? Tell me what Mr. Lopez said to you, and what you said back."

Jessica: "He asked me why I wasn't doing the page."

Charlotte: "And what did you say?"

Jessica: "I didn't answer him, Mama . . . he was mad, and I didn't know what to <u>say</u>."

Charlotte: "Okay . . . tell <u>me</u>, then. Why weren't you doing your work?"

Jessica: "I didn't understand. I never understand the grammar pages, Mama. And it always makes Mr. Lopez mad at me."

Charlotte: "Jessica, in a situation like that, when your teacher asks you why you're not working, you say what you just said to me. Politely. You say, 'I'm not working because I don't understand how to do it.' And then you say, 'Would you help me, please?'"

Jessica: "But he'd get <u>mad</u> at me!"

Charlotte: "Maybe so. But <u>think</u>: When you didn't answer at all, he got mad at you anyway. Right? This way is better, Jessica. This way he knows that it's not because you're naughty, or lazy; this way you are doing your best to explain."

After Charlotte finishes discussing the conversational strategy —
which may take a while, since Jessica is new at this — she should
also try to find out what it is about the grammar lesson that's baf-
fling Jessica so, and why. She's more likely to do that if she hasn't
already decided that grammar is something she was never good at
and that Jessica probably won't be good at either.

In the scenario, Charlotte had two communication goals. First,
she wanted to make Jessica *feel* better. Second, she wanted to think
of something she could say to John Lopez so that *she* wouldn't have
to listen to his verbal abuse. She accomplished the first goal, and
probably would have managed the second as well; she doesn't have
the same reasons to be intimidated by Mr. Lopez that Jessica has.
She did what she was trying to do — but her goals were badly chosen.

Her first goal should have been to find out *what language was
used between Jessica and the teacher,* in as much detail as the child
could provide. Her second goal should have been to model for Jessica some examples of language that would have made things better, in order to build her daughter's skill and confidence for the next
such interaction. "Never mind" and "Don't worry about it" are
short-term help; what a child needs is the long-term help that comes
from knowing that when you face a problem again you will be better equipped to deal with it.

Step 4 Backup

A New Technique: Using the Sensory Modes

One of the sets of information stored in your internal grammar is a detailed classification of the English vocabulary in terms of *sensory modes*. Suppose you hear someone say, "I see exactly what you mean," or "She's the apple of my eye," or "You're not looking at it the way I do." You know *immediately* that those sentences are from Sight Mode, the vocabulary of the eye. You don't have to go look that information up anywhere. Similarly, you would recognize "That's music to my ears" and "That really rings a bell with me" as belonging to Hearing Mode. And you would instantly classify "You've put your finger right on the source of the problem" and "He really rubs me the wrong way" as coming from Touch Mode. You already do this classification automatically; to do it consciously and deliberately, you just need to *pay attention* to what other people are saying.

If someone speaks to you in French and you answer in Chinese, communication will be difficult. We all know that people prefer to communicate in their own language and are less likely to be tense and anxious if we honor that preference. In the same way, though on a much smaller scale, communication improves when we use the *sensory* vocabulary preferred by the person we're talking to. This is called *sensory mode matching.*

Whenever your communication goal is to encourage trust and good feeling in the language environment, one of your best strategies is to use this technique. Everybody has a preferred sensory mode; when someone else uses that mode, they feel more comfortable. They think, *Here's somebody who speaks my language . . . who perceives the world the way I do. Even if we disagree, this is somebody I can talk to.*

To take advantage of this fact about language, all you have to do is follow two simple rules:

1. Match the sensory mode coming at you if you can.

2. If you can't match modes, try not to use any sensory vocabulary at all.

Examples

Following Rule #1:

John: "How bad does it look?" (Sight Mode)
Mary: "I don't see it as anything very serious." (Sight Mode; this is sensory mode matching.)

Following Rule #2:

Mary: "How bad does it look?" (Sight Mode)
John: "I don't think it's anything very serious." (Neutral; no sensory vocabulary has been used.)

Breaking Both Rules:

John: "How does my idea sound to you?" (Hearing Mode)
Mary: "I don't feel as if you have a good grasp of the problem." (Touch Mode; this is sensory mode *mis*match.)

The backup pages that follow will help you put this technique to use in your own language environment.

Practicing Your Sensory Mode Skills

1. Make a sensory mode database. Set up a diary page in your verbal self-defense notebook for each of the three common sensory modes (sight, hearing, and touch), and keep a record of useful words, phrases, and sentences for each one. (Because our culture is heavily biased in favor of the eye and ear, you may find it harder to fill your page with touch examples.) Here are a few examples to get you started.

Sight Mode: I see what you mean; try to see it my way; it's not clear to me; point of view; it looks great; she was a sight for sore eyes; they didn't even blink once; look what you did.

Hearing Mode: That sounds terrific; it's just a lot of static to me; I hear what you're saying; the way I hear it, they're wrong; you're not listening; there's a lot of noise in that message; that doesn't ring true, somehow.

Touch Mode: I get it; that feels right to me; a slippery slope; she has all the information right at her fingertips; put your back into it; I don't care for rough talk; hold that thought.

2. Set up a diary page to do "translations" from one sensory mode to another. The more practice you get using all three sensory modes, the easier it will be for you to do sensory mode matching. Here are some examples:

Hearing Mode: It's music to my ears.

  a. It's a perfect picture to me. (Sight Mode translation.)

  b. It's as smooth as velvet to me. (Touch Mode translation.)

Touch Mode: Let's try to stay in touch.

  a. Let's try to see each other more often. (Sight Mode translation.)

  b. I'd like to hear from you more often. (Hearing Mode translation.)

It's important to remember what translation really is. You don't translate an English sentence into Navajo by substituting a Navajo word for each English word and changing the order of the words to fit the Navajo grammar rules. You do it by finding the Navajo sentence that a native speaker of Navajo would have used in the same situation where *you* would have used the English sentence.

3. Find out which is your *own* preferred sensory mode.

  a. Try keeping a record of the sensory language you hear yourself use, for two or three weeks.

  b. Try to answer this question: When you're tense or upset, which sensory-system vocabulary are you most likely to rely on? (Ask family members to help you with this; often they can tell you the answer right away.)

  c. In a stressful situation, which are you most likely to say?

    "It looks to me like you're not even willing to try!"
    "You don't sound like you're even willing to try!"
    "I don't feel like you're even willing to try!"

"I don't see what you mean; it's not clear at all."
"I hear you, but what you're saying sounds all
   mixed up to me."
"I just don't get what you're saying at all."

d. How do you learn best? By looking at information, or by listening to it? By getting in there with both hands and working with it? Your preference will be reflected in your language choices, especially when you're upset or under stress.

4. Now, using the questions in skill number 3, find out the preferred sensory modes of people that you talk with on a regular basis—members of your household, people at your workplace, your close friends, and so forth. A list of these preferences can be a tremendous help to you in reducing hostility and increasing understanding in your language environment.

If there's a particular person that you seem *always* to have communication problems with, investigate the possibility that the two of you consistently use different sensory modes. This is a common source of misunderstanding and communication breakdown.

One More Look at Scenario Four

Using your new information about the sensory modes, go back to Scenario Four and take a good look at the interaction between Jessica and her teacher. Then set up a diary page to complete the three questions below.

1. Which sensory mode does Jessica use most consistently?

2. Which sensory mode does Mr. Lopez use most consistently?

3. Rewrite the dialogue between these two as it would have sounded if one of them had followed the sensory mode rules on page 95.

◆

If either Jessica or the teacher had known how to use the sensory mode technique, their communication would have been much less hostile, because people who are under stress tend to become *locked in* to their preferred sensory mode. The more frightened Jessica became, and the angrier John Lopez grew, the more their different sensory mode preferences interfered with their attempts to communicate.

Sensory Mode Mismatch Incident Log

The goal of this diary page is to record some language interactions where sensory mode mismatch occurs, along with the consequences. (These can be personal interactions, or dialogue that you overhear. You may also get interesting examples from television or other media.)

DATE: _____

DESCRIPTION OF THE SITUATION:

WHAT ONE PERSON SAID, IN SIGHT/HEARING/TOUCH MODE:

WHAT THE OTHER PERSON SAID, IN SIGHT/HEARING/TOUCH MODE:

WHAT WAS SAID NEXT:

(Repeat as many times as necessary to record the conversation.)

HOW IT ALL TURNED OUT—THE CONSEQUENCES:

SOME THINGS THAT COULD HAVE BEEN SAID, TO AVOID THE SENSORY MODE MISMATCH:

COMMENTS:

Sensory Mode Matching Incident Log

The goal of this diary page is to record some language interactions where sensory mode matching occurs, along with the consequences. (These can be personal interactions, or dialogue that you overhear. You may also get interesting examples from television or other media.)

DATE: _____

DESCRIPTION OF THE SITUATION:

WHAT ONE PERSON SAID, IN SIGHT/HEARING/TOUCH MODE:

WHAT THE OTHER PERSON SAID, IN SIGHT/HEARING/TOUCH MODE:

WHAT WAS SAID NEXT:

(Repeat as many times as necessary to record the conversation.)

HOW IT ALL TURNED OUT—THE CONSEQUENCES:

COMMENTS:

✦ SIGHT BITES ✦
Quotations to Think About and Use

ON SHORT-TERM SOLUTIONS

"[W]hat we need in a universe such as ours are not rocks and bastions; we need the knowledge of how to float and swim."

(Watts 1967, p. 115.)

ON LANGUAGE LEARNING

"It is almost a conditioned reflex for Americans to approach the study of the workings of their language with reluctance, not to say downright distaste . . . But the biggest problem of all seems to be a matter of self-defense in the face of what is assumed by most students to be their inevitable . . . failure to deal with the subject adequately, no matter how hard they try."

(Herndon 1976, p. 301.)

"Ten linguists working full time for ten years to analyze the structure of the English language could not program a computer with the ability for language acquired by an average child in the first ten or even five years of life."

(Moskowitz, "The Acquisition of Language," in Clark et al. 1981, p. 78.)

"Whatever the built-in properties the brain brings to the task of language learning may be, it is now known that a child who hears no language learns no language, and that a child learns only the language spoken in her environment."

(Moskowitz, "Acquisition," in Clark et al. 1981, p. 82.)

"Language is not really something the child does; it is something that happens to the child placed in an appropriate environment, much as the child's body grows and matures in a predetermined way when provided with appropriate nutrition and environmental stimulation."

(N. Chomsky, quoted in Albert 1988, pp. 101–2.)

Understanding the Two Goals of Verbal Self-Defense

*Because verbal violence is at the root of all other
violence, I know what I must do to restore peace
in my life. I must do two things. I must create a
language environment where verbal abuse is truly
rare. And when I do find myself involved in verbal
violence, I must end it quickly and honorably
and put it firmly behind me.*

Scenario Five

Like any rheumatologist, Bradley Taylor had many patients with
chronic illnesses that caused them significant discomfort and for
whom there wasn't much he could do to help. The patient he was
seeing this morning was a good example. At fifty-seven, Moira
Carter had arthritis severe enough to give her a lot of pain in rainy
weather and mild discomfort the rest of the time, but it wasn't the
kind of rheumatic disease that justifies heroic measures.

Nevertheless, Miss Carter was in Dr. Taylor's office again — for
the third time this month — demanding that he find a way to make
her feel better.

"There has to be something you can do for me, Bradley Taylor,"
she was saying. Again.

Dr. Taylor looked up from the page of notes he was writing and
sighed deeply. He laid her file down on his desk, closing it carefully.
He put the cap on his pen and laid it down beside the file. He rubbed
the bridge of his nose with one forefinger, his eyes briefly closed.

Then he steepled his fingers, and looked at his patient over the top of them, eyebrows raised and lips narrowed. It was time, in his opinion, to bring some plain facts firmly and clearly to her attention.

"I insist," Moira Carter went on, filling the silence. "All this talk about the wonders of modern medicine! I just don't believe that nothing can be done."

"Miss Carter."

"Yes, Doctor?"

"You are not the only patient I HAVE, you know!"

Moira Carter looked startled. "Pardon me?"

"I said: you are not my only patient! Many of my patients, Miss Carter, aren't able to come to my office and demand that I work miracles. They can't even get out of their beds, you see. Not without help. They can't dress themselves. They can't hold a comb or brush, Miss Carter. They can't feed themselves. And they have nothing at all to look forward to, Miss Carter, but more of the same. YOU, on the other hand — as I have explained to you many times — are able to get around and go on with your life — and you have no reason to believe that your arthritis will ever be much more severe than it is right now. You are a very FORtunate WOman, Miss Carter!"

There was a long pause, while he looked at her sternly, waiting; and then she answered him. "I see. Thank you, doctor. I will certainly make an effort to remember all of that."

"There is one thing YOU could do, however," Dr. Taylor continued, glad to observe that he was getting his point across and that she wasn't going to persist in her endless complaining. "As I've told you before, you'd feel a lot better if — "

"If I'd lose weight," she said, cutting him off in mid-sentence.

"Exactly," he agreed.

"Eat less. Exercise more."

"Right again!"

To the doctor's astonishment, Moira Carter stood up without another word, and she sailed out of his office and through the reception area without even stopping at the front desk to pay her bill. He heard the nurse calling her name, but there was no answer. And then he heard the sound of Miss Carter's car leaving his parking lot in a way that could only be described as roaring out of the lot.

When Charlotte peered in his office door, looking puzzled, Dr. Taylor spoke first.

"Charlotte," he asked, "What on earth could I possibly have <u>said</u> to that woman to set her <u>off</u> like that???"

Charlotte gave him her most noncommital smile.

"I have no idea, Doctor," she said. "I'm sure it wasn't your fault. You know how arthritis patients are — when they're hurting, they get a little touchy."

He sighed, and shrugged his shoulders. "<u>Oh</u> well," he said. "Who's next, Charlotte?"

✦

What's Going On Here?

Bradley Taylor's Point of View

Bradley Taylor considers himself a good and caring and compassionate doctor. He knows chronic illness can be wearing even when it's not severe. He tries to keep that in mind; he tries never to allow himself to become annoyed with patients who find their problems hard to cope with. He would never deliberately talk to a patient abusively. But he believes that you have to be *firm* with patients. You can't let them get into the habit of going on and on about things that can't be helped. It's not good for them to dwell on their problems, and it wastes the doctor's valuable time; it can't be allowed.

In Moira Carter's case, he feels that it's important for her to understand that compared to many arthritis patients she has it easy. He wants her to understand that she doesn't have to worry about her disease progressing and putting *her* into a wheelchair or an invalid's bed. He feels an obligation to make this clear to her and to be absolutely sure she understands, so that she will have a wholesome attitude toward her illness and won't make things worse by a lot of unnecessary self-coddling and obsessing over symptoms. His goal is to tell patients the facts, straight out, without treating them like children, and that is exactly what he did with Miss Carter. As for her weight, it annoys him greatly that she won't lose the twenty pounds he has advised her to lose. That *would* make her life easier, by taking some of the burden off her bones and joints. He sees no reason why she should react angrily when he points it out to her; it's part of his job as a doctor to advise her about her lifestyle as it affects her health.

Moira Carter's Point of View

Miss Carter doesn't believe that she's being unreasonable when she asks Dr. Taylor to try to find a way to make her more comfortable; after all, that's part of his job as a doctor. If it's really true that he can't do anything more for her, she will stop asking—but she's not convinced. She constantly hears about new developments, new treatments, new drugs . . . how is *she* to know whether one of those might be helpful to her? Obviously the doctor won't keep looking for a new approach to her problem if he thinks she's satisfied with things as they are. It's her obligation as a patient to make sure he knows she's *not* satisfied.

She would find it difficult to explain clearly why she became so angry with Dr. Taylor during their latest meeting. She knows that every word he said is true. Many of his arthritis patients *are* far worse off than she is; they do have the problems he described; and she knows it's true that she's fortunate not to be in their situation. Furthermore, she understands that losing twenty pounds *would* be good for her joints. She doesn't disagree with any of the doctor's statements. *But it wasn't what he said—it was the <u>way</u> he said it!* She couldn't explain (which is why she didn't speak up on the spot), but she *knows* that Dr. Taylor wasn't just stating facts. She could tell . . . he was doing his best to make her feel *guilty*. She resents that bitterly. She will pay his bill when it arrives, but she has decided to change doctors. It's bad enough putting up with arthritis without having to put up with a guilt-tripping doctor too.

Charlotte's Point of View

Charlotte knows that Bradley Taylor's bedside manner leaves much to be desired and that his sharp tongue can also be turned on his employees. Her basic strategy for dealing with him is to stay out of his way. When that fails and she finds herself involved in one of his confrontations, she chooses her words carefully—to please him if she can, and to avoid angering him further if she can't.

✦

The scenario shows a communication breakdown very common in our society. About three-fourths of all patients who change doctors (and a sizable percentage of those who *sue* doctors) do so not because of some action the doctor takes but because of the doctor's words and the manner in which they're spoken. The problem in malpractice suits isn't medical error, most of the time, but Malpractice Of The Mouth. It's rare for the doctor to understand what caused the breakdown; the medical curriculum has yet to make room for courses in linguistics. Since doctors rarely shout open insults and obscenities at patients, their tendency is to protest with, "But all I said was . . ." And most patients, like Miss Carter, are ill equipped to explain what made them feel so hurt or so angry.

Why It Matters: The Link between Verbal and Physical Violence

We can't always avoid verbal violence; it's not possible. Like tornadoes and ticks and taxes, like forest fires and flu, verbal violence will come along from time to time and we will have to deal with it. We *can* keep it to a bare minimum. If we are verbal abusers we can do our best not to *create* verbal violence; if we are verbal victims or involved bystanders, we can do our best not to participate in verbal violence initiated by others. Still, there undoubtedly will be times when, despite our best efforts, we'll find ourselves faced with an episode of abusive language. When that happens, we need to know what to do to put an end to the episode — with no loss of face on either side of the confrontation.

Physical violence is at epidemic levels in our society today. For many parts of the population it is the major cause of injury; for some (teenage males, for example) it is also the leading cause of death. Physical violence overloads our emergency medicine departments and our legal systems; it is seriously endangering education in this country. It would be hard to overstate the seriousness of the problem, not only because of its direct effects but because the huge amounts of money we have to spend dealing with violence can't be spent in more constructive ways. But in our concern with such matters as locks and fences and metal detectors and stiffer sentences and gun control we have lost sight of the one thing that all types of physical violence have in common:

✦ Physical violence begins, 99 times out of 100, with *verbal* violence.

Normal people don't just walk up to others and start hitting — first, there are angry words. (Criminals, and people who suffer from the rare mental disorders that have violence as a prominent symptom, may hit first, of course; but few of the people we deal with every day will fall into those categories.) The problem is that the violence *escalates* along with the anger, from the first irritating (or irritated) remark to the final kick or blow to the head, or the final gunshot. Once the hitting starts, it's too late to save the situation; at that point we have to turn to law enforcement. But while the hostility is still being expressed in language, we still have the time and opportunity to set things right ourselves.

Verbal abuse doesn't usually come at us in the form of primitive hack-and-slash verbiage such as, "SHUT YOUR STUPID MOUTH, you obnoxious CREEP!" Most adults do very little verbal abuse of that kind, in spite of what you might think from watching television. When that *does* happen, it tends to be in the final stages of a terrible fight that has escalated out of control. Such language is as close to physical abuse as you can get without actually hitting; more often than not, it *accompanies* physical abuse and is part of a physical (rather than verbal) violence pattern.

What we more often find ourselves facing or using, instead of open epithets and obscenities, is much more subtle verbal attacks, where the problem often isn't in the *words* that are said. In many cases, like that of Moira Carter in Scenario Five, the victims of such abuse can't explain how they *know* they're under attack.

It's easy to explain your negative reaction when you can say, "I'm angry because you told me to shut my stupid mouth and called me an obnoxious creep." When it's like that, you can make your objections clear to the attacker and you can reasonably expect sympathy from anyone you describe the incident to. It's much harder to do this when you can't find the provocation in the words themselves. But it's not impossible. And it's critically important if we are ever to get our lives in order.

What to Do about It:
Recognizing Abusive Language

The Melody of English Anger

A language feature that contributes heavily to the creation of hostility in English is the use of strong emphasis (*acoustic stress*) on words and parts of words. Suppose someone asks you, "Why are you leaving?" That's a neutral question. The speaker is just interested in the information and is requesting that you provide it. But those same four words can be said in ways that are *not* neutral. For example:

1. "<u>Why</u> are you leaving?"
2. "WHY are you leaving?"
3. "WHY are you LEAVing?"
4. "WHY ARE YOU LEAVing?"
5. "WHY are YOU LEAVing?"

The first example isn't neutral, but it's not necessarily hostile. The speaker is stressing "why" to express an emotion . . . it could be annoyance, but it could also be tender concern, anxiety, curiosity, or mild distress. The other four examples, however, are hostile speech.

When we say examples 2–5 out loud, putting extra stress (emphasis) on the parts written all in capital letters, that tune we hear is the melody of English ANGER. The question isn't neutral anymore; the person asking doesn't just want information. The difference between "why" and "WHY" is more than just loudness and pitch.

✦ "Why" means: *You have the information that is the answer to this question; I'm asking you to share it with me; and I have the right to ask.*

✦ "WHY" means: *You have the information that is the answer to this question; I'm asking you to share it with me; I have the right to ask; and I'm telling you in advance:* <u>Whatever</u> *your answer is, it's not* <u>good</u> *enough!!"*

Much of the verbal abuse we deal with in everyday life is like the examples on page 110, made up of ordinary words that have been made hostile by extra emphatic stresses. And this is a factor over which it's possible for us to have some measure of control.

Two situations in English require extra emphatic stress that has nothing to do with hostility. One is *contrastive stress,* used when we need to contrast two or more items for clarity, as in "It wasn't the <u>dog</u> that dug up the flower beds, it was the <u>cat</u>!" or "I didn't buy that car in Ju<u>ly</u>, I bought it in <u>March</u>." The other is what we might call *"announcement" stress,* used when we need to convey a message of extreme excitement, as in "Look OUT for that TRUCK!" or "SOMEbody just MUGGED me!" or "HEY, your MOTHER just won the LOTTery!"

We recognize contrastive stress and the "announcement" variety easily. We're not likely to mistake them for verbal abuse. But when we hear any other type of English with extra emphatic stresses, we tend to add the same kind of stresses to our response. This is our way of conveying the message that we *hear* hostility and we don't like it. It's natural and normal, but it has serious potential drawbacks. We mean it as a *warning.* When it functions that way, causing the other person to tone down his or her language, that's fine. Much of the time, however, that's not what happens, especially when the language interaction involves people who perceive themselves as equals. Remember: ANYTHING YOU FEED WILL GROW.

Think of what happens when somebody you don't feel free to fuss at talks to you too loudly. You answer a little more loudly than you would ordinarily talk . . . and the person answers more loudly still . . . and that makes you talk more loudly too . . . until the two of you are shouting at each other. The same thing happens when you answer one utterance that's marked with extra stresses by using another utterance of the same kind. That's the melody of anger going both ways, anger feeding anger; it sets up a hostility loop, and it will grow.

Whether we are verbal abusers or verbal victims, we need to

begin paying careful attention to the *tune* we're setting our words to. Whether we are starting the conversation or responding to someone else's opening line, we can be careful not to add the extra stresses that signal hostility.

✦ WARNING: Some people routinely speak with a more monotonous or more varied intonation than others do. Sometimes this is a personal characteristic; sometimes it's part of the grammar of their dialect. When we talk about "extra" emphatic stresses, we have to remember that we mean "extra *for that person.*" If the person is a stranger, we may make a mistake and perceive hostility where none exists, or vice versa. With people we talk to often, however, we can tell when the number of stresses and their intensity are greater than is usual for that individual. We just need to pay attention.

"You and I; You and Me"

A second characteristic of hostile language is that it's intensely personal, heavily peppered with "I, me, my, mine, myself, we, us, our, ours, ourselves, you, your, yours, yourself, yourselves," and "this." As in "I don't understand why you never consider MY feelings!" and "If you REALLY loved us, YOU wouldn't WANT us to be miserable!" and "THIS time you've REALLY blown it!" There are other kinds of "I/me/you" language that aren't hostile, of course; "I love you" is an excellent example. But we can tell the difference between the very personal language of intimacy and romance and the very personal language of verbal abuse, because:

✦ Almost always, language that has *both* of the characteristics just discussed — *extra emphatic stress on words and parts of words* plus *heavy use of "I/me/you" vocabulary* — is hostile language.

The exceptions — which will occur because of a need to express contrast or astonishment — will be obvious to you because you are a speaker of English and because the situation they occur in will make them clear. You won't mistake a sincere and enthusiastic "But

I <u>don't</u> just LIKE you! I LOVE you!" or "But WE want YOU, not Mr. WILLiams, to be the captain of OUR team!" for verbal abuse.

Examples

Once again, we can take an active step to keep the hostility we hear from escalating, by refusing to feed the loop: by answering the personal language with *im*personal language. Compare these two dialogues.

DIALOGUE ONE: *Answering Hostility with Hostility*

Tracy: "WHY can't you EVER put anything aWAY where it GOES? I don't have TIME to pick up after you!"

Lee: "What do you MEAN, you have to pick up after me? You DO NOT! I DO put things back where they're supposed to be!"

Tracy: "Oh, YEAH? Then WHY can't I find the SCISsors? YOU had them LAST, you know!"

DIALOGUE TWO: *Short-Circuiting Hostility*

Tracy: "WHY can't you EVER put anything aWAY where it GOES? I don't have TIME to pick up after you!"

Lee: "It's really irritating when things aren't where they belong."

Tracy: "It sure is! I can't find the scissors, and I really need them. Do you know where they are?"

In Dialogue One, Tracy sets up one end of the hostility loop by opening a conversation with language that's full of personal words and extra emphatic stresses — and Lee comes right back with language of the same kind, which feeds the loop. Tracy's next utterance is as hostile as the first one, and these two people are headed for a fight.

In Dialogue Two, Lee responds to Tracy's abusive language with a statement that is free of either personal language or extra stresses, that is appropriate for the situation, and that does nothing at all to feed the hostility loop. Tracy's next utterance is then *less* hostile and the fight is no longer probable. Said neutrally, Lee's sentence short-circuits the hostility loop *using a statement that both Tracy and Lee can agree with,* and it doesn't require Lee to sacrifice either principles or dignity. No loss of face occurs on either side.

It's very important for Lee to be *sure* that sentence is neutral. Suppose it sounds like this . . .

> "It's REALly IRRitating when THINGS aren't where they beLONG!"

That's a counterattack. The words are the same, but the tune isn't; the words have to be said without those extra stresses.

✦ WARNING: It's also important to avoid using a technique that is often recommended in materials on communication, in which you respond by summing up what the speaker said to you. If Lee used that technique in the dialogue the line would be, "You feel that you have to pick up after me and that I don't put things away properly." This technique may be useful for therapists and counselors; almost everywhere else, it's only infuriating.

Suppose Lee *doesn't* feel irritated when things are out of place, and could not sincerely say, "It's really irritating when . . ." In that case, there's an equally useful alternative:

> "Lots of people really find it irritating when things aren't where they belong."

Tracy may answer with "Right! And I'm <u>one</u> of them!"; that's far better than the inevitable angry response to "I DO TOO put things where they belong!" The "Lots of people . . ." sentence is something both Lee and Tracy can agree on; it's not verbal abuse, or pleading, or an attempt to reason with Tracy; and it does not feed the hostility loop Tracy was trying to set up.

Now we can summarize this information.

1. To Recognize Hostile Language and Verbal Abuse:

✦ Listen for extra stresses on words and parts of words, and —
especially in the same sequence of language — frequent use of
personal words like "I/me/you/your/we/us."

2. To Defuse the Hostility and Respond Effectively:

✦ Never feed the verbal violence loop: Answer without extra
stresses, using neutral intonation and impersonal language.

Our internal grammars contain all the rules for using language
this way. We already know how to do it; we have the necessary
skills. We just have to focus on three goals:

a. We have to resist the temptation to fall into the old habit of
being "right" at all costs even when we don't really care about
the issue, even when it causes us (or others) pain.

b. We have to resist the temptation to participate in verbal violence
loops because "It's fun!" or because that's how we've always
handled conflict in the past.

c. We have to *pay attention* to our own language and the language
we hear and observe.

Finally, it's important to notice that nowhere in the information
about recognizing hostile language is there any instruction to watch
out for hostile *words. No word is inherently hostile in and of itself.*
The personal pronouns ("I/me/you," etc.) are not inherently hostile.
Even obscenities and ethnic epithets, ugly and unpleasant as they
are in the majority of cases, *can* be used without hostility. We need
to always be alert to the possibility that the "positive" words someone is saying are actually verbal abuse, while the "negative" words
said by someone else may be rude or tactless but are not verbal
abuse at all. We need to be careful not to give excessive importance
to words.

The emphasis our society places on the need for "a powerful

vocabulary" has its place. When you write instructions for assembling a machine, or directions for finding a lake, or when you draw up a legal contract, word choice can be critical. For any sequence of *written* language, word choice matters a great deal, because most of the information carried by body language (especially the tone and intonation of the voice) is missing. English punctuation does a poor job of letting us know how written language would sound if spoken aloud. But for the expression of feelings and emotions in speech, the focus on vocabulary is an error. Many of the things "everybody knows" are false, but this one is absolutely true:

✦ IT'S NOT WHAT YOU SAY, IT'S THE WAY YOU SAY IT.

Another Look at Scenario Five

There's nothing specifically offensive or abusive about the words Bradley Taylor used to Miss Carter. A physician is expected to provide useful information about what a patient is doing wrong and should be doing instead, with regard to health and well-being. We go to doctors to get personal advice and criticism that we would probably resent from almost anyone else. Dr. Taylor's communication problem is not in his choice of words but in the melody he sets them to. For example, he says to Moira Carter:

"You're not the only patient I HAVE, you know!"

The words are true and accurate. They are a valid way to remind Miss Carter that the doctor has many patients who have claims on his time and attention and that when she keeps coming in to ask him for things he can't give her, she is taking time away from those other patients. If he had used neutral intonation — if he had said, "You're not the only patient I have, you know" — the line would not have been verbal abuse. It might have been tactless, and it was surely not the best possible way to word the message, but it would not have been abuse. The problem is the extra stresses on "you're" and "only" and "have."

The doctor goes on for the rest of the interaction, not only using very personal language — which is appropriate between doctor and patient — but combining the personal language with frequent extra stresses on words and parts of words, which isn't. Sometimes the stress is light, as in "Many of my patients aren't able to come to my office . . ."; sometimes it's heavy, as in "YOU, on the other hand . . ."; sometimes he mixes the stress levels, as in "There is one thing YOU could do . . ." A doctor who is advising a patient can get away with a few such extra stresses, carefully placed. But a consistent pattern like Bradley Taylor's is Malpractice Of The Mouth. Miss Carter is entirely justified in taking offense.

If Bradley Taylor were taken to task for abusing Moira Carter, he would undoubtedly point out that he had "only said" the following:

- That he had many patients whose condition was worse than hers, even to the point of causing grave disability.

- That she need not worry about her illness progressing in that way.

- That it would be best for her to remember these things, in order to keep a sense of proportion.

- That she would probably be more comfortable if she weighed twenty pounds less.

And he would be able to say, accurately, that not one *word* of that was either false or offensive, or inappropriate between a doctor and a patient. In such a situation, only one response would constitute verbal self-defense. Here it is:

> "Dr. Taylor, two defining characteristics of abusive language in English are the frequent use of very personal language — which is permitted to physicians — and the frequent use of unnecessary extra acoustic stresses on words and parts of words, which is not. The words you used were not abusive in themselves, but they were made abusive by your intonation."

As long as our educational system fails to provide us with the information that would make a statement like that possible for the average person, the chances of any doctor hearing it are close to zero.

A Brief Word about Nonverbal Communication and Children

Recent research has given us solid evidence that many children who are unpopular with other kids, who have trouble fitting in, and who are called "weird" by their peers, have serious problems with body language. They have trouble using nonverbal communication to get their *own* messages across accurately, and they either miss or misunderstand body language signals coming from other children. This can be a grave handicap, and it needs urgent attention.

Children do get explicit training in "which words to use," if not at home, then in the classroom. The training may not be perfect, but it's there. The explicit information that children are given about body language, however, is often limited to rules of etiquette, as in "Stand up straight when you're talking to your grandmother!" and "Don't scratch yourself in public!" and "Don't yell at people!"

Because children are able to learn their grammar *without* explicit and open instruction, we can be reasonably certain that those whose body language causes them problems have learned their nonverbal grammar from poor or inadequate models. The most useful thing that parents and other caregivers can do for such children is to improve their *own* body language skills, so that they provide the children around them with a model that doesn't lead them astray.

Step 5 Backup

---◆---

Hostile Language/Verbal Abuse Log

Set up a diary page to record examples of hostile language and verbal abuse that you encounter in your daily life. Record your examples in as much detail as you can. Include the body language that you observed at the time, remembering that tone of voice and intonation are the most *powerful* parts of nonverbal communication. It's also useful to record facial expressions, postures, and gestures that accompany verbal abuse. For each example you record, do two things:

1. Underline the extra stresses that you heard on words and parts of words, or write them in capital letters.

2. Circle the instances of personal "I/you/this family/this office" language.

DATE: _____

DESCRIPTION OF THE SITUATION:

HOSTILE LANGUAGE THAT WAS USED:

(Example: "Can't you EVER get to work on TIME? There are OTHER people in this office who'd like to sleep late TOO, you know!")

COMMENTS:

◆ NOTE: You might also find it useful, as a way of improving your skill at recognizing hostility in others' speech, to set up a diary page to record and analyze hostile language you hear on television. Be sure you work with programs that offer at least roughly normal speech, rather than game shows, talk shows that offer *only* hostile language, and the like. The TV set is always available to you for this sort of practice, at your convenience. And unlike a living person, it won't be offended or puzzled when you take notes on the conversation.

Techniques for Getting Control of Your Own Intonation

1. *Using the Tape Recorder.* Many people aren't consciously aware of how often they use extra stresses—that is, stresses not needed for comparison or "announcement"—on words and parts of words. To find out whether you fall into this "unaware" group, spend some time recording yourself in conversation (with the permission of the others present, of course). Make recordings that are long enough to let you get past the stage of being self-conscious about being taped. Listen to the tapes to find out what your own intonation is like; if you don't feel that you can be objective about this, ask someone you trust to listen and give you her opinion.

✦ NOTE: These extra stresses aren't found just in the language of people launching verbal attacks. They're also characteristic of the speech of verbal victims, and they are very commonly present in pleading and attempts at "logical argument."

2. *Speaking in Melodies.* There's a classic technique taught by voice teachers and drama coaches that you can use as a way to bring the intonation of your voice under your conscious control. It's not something you'd want to do in public, and it's not easy—but it works. Here are the steps you follow:

   a. Choose a simple familiar tune like "Three Blind Mice."

   b. Now *say* the tune—don't sing it. That is, say it out loud, changing the pitch of your voice as it changes in the song, but don't let yourself switch from speaking to singing. (Don't worry about the *rhythm* of the song! You may have to do this extremely slowly, and it may take you a long time to make some of the pitch changes. Just concentrate on the pitches.)

c. When you can do simple tunes easily, move on to more complicated ones.

No matter how badly you do this, it will still help. It trains your ears to *hear* pitches of the voice. And it helps you become familiar with the way the muscles of your mouth and tongue and throat *feel* at various pitches. It gives you the kind of feedback that's essential to learning.

3. *Visualizing the Sound of Your Speech.* Start talking, on any subject at all, in private. As you talk, imagine that the words you're saying are coming out of your mouth as a supple *ribbon* of sound that you can actually see in the air. (Make the image in the way most useful to you . . . see the words as written on a strip of paper, or a strip of velvet, or just see them as one letter after another floating in the air . . . whatever works for *you*.) Try to make the ribbon go up . . . go down . . . trace patterns in the air . . . stay level. You may find it useful to use your tape recorder as you do this and then listen to the tape as a way of getting additional feedback.

When you feel that you can do this well, try it while you're actually talking to other people, keeping the sound path appropriate for the language that you're using.

✦ NOTE: As you do #2 and #3, pay close attention to the way your vocal muscles feel. Pay attention to the way you breathe. Try to become consciously aware of the pitch and tone and quality of your voice, so that when you're talking in the real world and can't constantly monitor these things, the system will be on "automatic pilot."

✦ SIGHT BITES ✦
Quotations to Think About and Use

ON USING HOSTILE LANGUAGE

"Words bruise and batter on the inside like physical blows bruise and lacerate the skin. That's why it's called *verbal abuse.* We're often unaware of the damage our words cause because we can't see the inner cuts and bruises."

(Wright 1991, p. 26.)

"It is possible to say approximately the same thing in any number of different ways."

(Renkema 1993, p. 97.)

ON BODY LANGUAGE

"How a judge gives his instructions to a jury was perceived to double the likelihood that the jury would deliver a verdict of guilty or not guilty — even when on the surface the judge's demeanor seemed perfectly impartial . . . When videotapes were analyzed by independent raters, they found that the judges' tone of voice, rather than anything in their words or body movements, communicated the strongest, most negative messages."

(Goleman 1986.)

"For many children, it's not what they say in words; it's the way they communicate non-verbally that shuts them out."

(Kochakian 1992.)

"[T]oddlers often imitate the distress of someone else — apparently, researchers say, in an effort to better understand what the other person is feeling. This kind of imitation, called 'motor mimicry,' was the original meaning of the word 'empathy' . . ."

(Goleman 1989.)

"Since most of the emotional messages sent between people are communicated nonverbally — by a gesture or tone of voice, say — the inability to read or send such messages adeptly is a major social handicap . . ."

(Goleman 1989.)

"No one knows just what internal mechanism governs social rhythms, but researchers are finding that a finely tuned sense of rhythmic synchrony . . . may play a crucial role in our ability to talk to each other, to work with one another, even to fall and stay in love."

— and —

"'You can see a family or group of friends separate itself out from a crowd after two or three film frames,' says Edward T. Hall, an anthropologist . . . 'They'll share their own rhythm and move in rhythmic synchrony.'"

(Douglas 1987, pp. 37–38, 42.)

ON VIOLENCE IN OUR SOCIETY

"In the 1990s, 'dissin' is fast becoming a national pastime. Cutting insults, crude put-downs and vulgar and vicious personal lampoons are dominating mainstream entertainment . . . More than ever, comedy draws the most laughs when it's at the expense of someone else."

(Easton 1993.)

"The adolescent population is the only age group in America with an increasing mortality rate during the past 25 years. Violence remains the leading cause of adolescent deaths, with accidents, suicides, and homicides accounting for more than 75% of teenage mortality."

(Greydanus 1987, p. 2110.)

"Every 12 seconds a woman is beaten by someone she knows — a husband, boyfriend, or relative. An estimated 30 percent of women seen in emergency rooms have been battered . . . But there are lots of women who are not physically beaten; rather, they are emotionally beaten."

(Phillips 1992, p. 48DD.)

"In our contemporary U.S. society, interpersonal violence is perhaps the most dangerous and rapidly increasing form of death and injury that we know . . . Violent deaths are the largest cause of mortality in the United States for more than half of the normal life span . . ."

(Check 1985, p. 721.)

◆

Deciding Never to Participate in Verbal Violence— And Following Through

*Because verbal abuse is impossible to do alone,
I know how to begin creating the language
environment I need. From now on, I refuse
to serve as a partner — either as victim or
as abuser — in verbal violence.*

Scenario Six

"Well, if it's not Counselor <u>She</u>ridan!" Jerry said, grinning at his sis-ter-in-law. "Tell me . . . to <u>what</u> do we owe <u>this</u> honor?"

Charlotte tensed; bracing herself for a scene had become a reflex for her after nine years with Jerry. She hadn't expected him to have time to come home before he went to his Kiwanis meeting, and she was sorry to find herself mistaken. But then she remembered, and relaxed. This wasn't just <u>anybody</u> Jerry was baiting, this was her <u>sis</u>-ter! She smiled, and poured glasses of lemonade all around.

"It's this porch, Jerry," Geneva Sheridan answered. "No matter how hot it is, this porch always has a cool breeze. I can't resist it."

"And I thought it was my <u>charm</u> that dragged you out of the courtroom, Geneva!" he said. "I'm <u>hurt</u>."

"Lawyers are immune to charm. Fortunately. It's a course they take in law school — Immunity 101."

Jerry laughed, and leaned back in the big wicker chair to drink his lemonade, while Geneva told them about the case she was working on right now.

Charlotte listened, fascinated; the doctor that Geneva's client was suing sounded like a clone of Bradley Taylor.

"It seems to me, Gen," she began, "that the — "

But Jerry cut her off sharply.

"Oh, come on, Charlotte!" he said. "Let her finish! So you're a nurse . . . that doesn't make you an expert on malpractice."

"I wasn't claiming to be an expert, Jerry," Charlotte protested.

"Sure you were!"

"I was not! You sound just like your mother, you know that?"

Jerry laughed, but it was a sarcastic laugh this time. "I'm sorry, Geneva," he said, with mock politeness. "You might as well forget about finishing your story. You can't say two words about anything medical around here without Nurse Charlotte grabbing the floor."

Geneva nodded. "People are very interested in the health care system," she said gravely. "It's not like contract law, or a boundary squabble. It's part of everybody's life, and what happens in medicine matters to people." She leaned toward Jerry. "What do you think — are we going to end up with a national health care system in this country or not?"

Jerry made a face. "I hope not," he said. "That's all we need — a health care system that runs like the post office. On the other hand . . ."

Charlotte sat quietly while Jerry and Geneva took up the points for and against national health care, one by one, and discussed them. She would have liked to join in the discussion; it was a subject she cared about. But she wasn't about to risk setting Jerry off again. She stayed on the sidelines and let the others talk.

Later, when Jerry had left for his meeting and the two women were alone, Charlotte spoke up. "Do you suppose, Gen," she asked, "that if I'd gone to law school Jerry and I would be able to get through half an hour without fighting?"

"Is that a serious question?"

"Absolutely serious."

"It shouldn't be. Remember last fall, when I brought Nate Cleaver over here to meet Jerry? He's a lawyer, but remember what a disaster that was? He and Jerry fought the whole evening, and I had to fake a call from the office to get Nate out of here—I was scared they were going to start hitting each other. Remember?"

"I'd forgotten about that," Charlotte said. "It was <u>awful</u>."

"Mmhmm. Nate's like you . . . he lets people get to him."

"Geneva," Charlotte protested, "you can't just let people walk all <u>over</u> you! When Jerry comes at me the way he does, with all those smart cracks—surely you don't think I should just sit there and TAKE it!"

"Charlotte, honey—Jerry shouldn't talk to you the way he does, either in private or in front of other people. But he couldn't <u>do</u> it if you weren't so eager to help him along."

"That's <u>not fair</u>, Geneva! How can you <u>say</u> that to me? <u>You</u> know how he <u>is</u>! You're my <u>sister</u>, for crying out loud! WHY aren't you on MY side?"

There was a long silence, and then Geneva said, "Charlotte, I'd like to stay and talk, but I think I'd better get myself together and head for home. I've got a deposition tomorrow at eight o'clock, and the traffic is going to be terrible."

What's Going On Here?

Jerry's Point of View

Jerry likes his sister-in-law. She's sharp, she's interesting to talk to, she's fun to be around. He's even gone to court a couple of times to watch her at work, and he was profoundly impressed by her performance as a trial lawyer. He wouldn't want to be *married* to her, however, and he's not surprised that she's still single. In Jerry's opinion, she's like a fancy resort—nice to visit, but you wouldn't want to be there all the time. He just wishes Charlotte would take a leaf or two from Geneva's book. Not the whole thing . . . he wants his wife to be someone who can look up to a man and build *his* self-confidence; he can't imagine Geneva Sheridan doing that. But he'd like Charlotte to be able to carry on an adult conversation without getting her feelings hurt all the time.

Geneva's Point of View

Geneva understands Jerry very well. He's insecure because he's stuck in a middle-management job with no chance for advancement, because he has a set of domineering parents who interfere in his life and refuse to treat either him or Charlotte as an adult, and because he's under stress all the time. She's sorry he's boxed in as he is; if she were Jerry she would quit the dead-end job, move away from the smothering parents, and get a *life*. But that's his business, and she doesn't intend to add an interfering sister-in-law to his burdens.

What she *doesn't* understand is Charlotte's behavior. Jerry's a bit of a bully, but his heart isn't in it; when you refuse to play his silly games, he backs down immediately. She knows he loves Charlotte and Jessica and Adam, and she has never found him hard to distract from his abusive tactics, the way he would be if he were actually a cruel man. Why Charlotte lets him sucker her into one fight after another is a mystery to Geneva.

She used to sit down with her sister and try to explain how to deal with Jerry. It never helped. Every single time, it ended with Charlotte angry or crying or both. Now Geneva's strategy is simple. As much as possible, she sees Charlotte only when Jerry isn't around; when she has to see the two of them together, she flatly refuses to be part of their fights; and she works hard at keeping her opinions about their relationship to herself.

Charlotte's Point of View

Charlotte is as baffled by Geneva's behavior as Geneva is by hers. There are three things she thinks her sister ought to do, and Geneva isn't doing *any* of them.

First, it seems to her that when Jerry starts attacking Charlotte, Geneva should *object*. After all, she's a trial lawyer, trained to use language for both attack and defense. She should be assertive enough to say something like, "Jerry, I don't think you should talk to Charlotte like that, especially not in front of other people." Something short and firm and to the point — so he would know that Charlotte isn't alone in her opinion of his abusive language.

Second, Charlotte wishes Geneva would take Jerry on and beat him at his own game once in a while, as she most certainly *could* do.

Finally, if her sister won't do either of those things for her, Charlotte feels that Geneva ought to at least teach *her* how to do them. She should share her knowledge and her strategies, so that Jerry wouldn't have it so easy. But every time she has asked Geneva for that kind of help, it seems to her that her sister has immediately started trying to put the blame on Charlotte. It's not fair; it's not right; and it *hurts*.

The Problem of Following Through

By the time you've reached Step 6, you will fully understand the basic principles of surviving — and eliminating — verbal abuse in your language environment, and you will have begun using a set of helpful verbal self-defense techniques. You want to succeed, and you're willing to make an investment of your time and energy; if that weren't true, you wouldn't be working your way through this program. But one difficult problem remains to be discussed, and by this point you will be very aware of its existence: It's the problem of *following through*. As with any other major change in your life, it's one thing to know what needs to be done; it's another to follow through and actually *do* it, even when you're well equipped for the task.

If You're a Verbal Victim

Verbal victims usually offer two explanations, both based on misunderstandings about verbal abuse, for the trouble they have in following through:

1. "I knew what I ought to do, and I understood why — but I just couldn't let him/her get <u>away</u> with it!"

2. "I knew what I ought to do, and I understood why — but I felt so guilty that I just couldn't <u>do</u> it!"

Let's discuss these two common barriers, one at a time.

The First Barrier: Fear of "Losing"

If you're a verbal victim, it's important for you to remember these facts about chronic verbal abusers.

- They use the melody of anger — but much of the time they're not angry when they begin the attack. (If they *are* angry, they're usually angry about something else, or with somebody else.)

- They ask questions — but they usually have no interest in the information they're asking for.

- They make statements — but they usually have no interest in the normal responses to those statements.

- They use verbal violence for just two purposes: to demonstrate their power to get and hold their victims' attention, and to provoke an emotional reaction that is additional evidence for that power.

✦ Letting verbal abusers' insults and smart cracks and hurtful remarks go by isn't letting them get away with it. Allowing them to succeed in their goal of tying up your attention and getting an emotional reaction from you *is* letting them get away with it.

Suppose your spouse says to you: "If you REALLY loved me, YOU wouldn't waste MONEY the way you do!" Hearing yourself accused of wasting money *hurts*. Your tendency is to respond in one of the three traditional ways.

1. With a counterattack.

    "LISTen, I don't waste HALF as much money as YOU do!"

    — or —

    "What do you MEAN? I do NOT waste money!"

2. By trying to debate, using logical arguments.

    "I don't think that's accurate. For example, let's consider what I spent on clothing this month, and compare it with . . ."

— or —

"If you're referring to the coat I bought yesterday, I want to remind you that I had several good <u>reasons</u> for buying that coat. First . . ."

3. By pleading.

"Honey, <u>please</u> don't start that! You KNOW how much it upsets me, and you KNOW how much work I have to do today! <u>Pleease</u> . . ."

Nothing could be more natural than these three reactions. But let's call on our common sense here. What do they actually accomplish? Simple . . .

✦ ALL THREE REACTIONS REWARD THE VERBAL ABUSER; ALL THREE FEED THE VERBAL VIOLENCE LOOP AND MAKE IT GROW.

You had a plan for your next half-hour; there were things you wanted to do and intended to do. Your spouse had a *different* plan for your time, in which you would give up your own plan and waste that time in a verbal confrontation. When that works — when you abandon your own plan and participate in the confrontation — your spouse is "getting away with it," and you're helping to make that possible.

Instead of doing that, you can ignore the obvious bait — the claim that you waste money — and respond to the *rest* of the attack, being careful not to put any extra emphatic stresses on words or parts of words. Like this:

Spouse: "If you REALLY loved me, YOU wouldn't waste MONEY the way you do!"

You: "When did you start thinking I don't love you?"

— or —

"Of course I love you; I love you very much."

These answers (which respond to "If you REALLY loved me" instead of to "YOU wouldn't waste MONEY the way you do!") *defuse* the verbal attack. They're not what the verbal abuser expects or wants to hear. They make it hard to set up a hostility loop and hard to go on with the attack. Said neutrally, they provide no emotional reaction to fuel a fight with.

And if the attack comes from a boss instead of a spouse? As in, "If you REALLY cared about this company, YOU wouldn't waste MONEY the way you do!"? You ignore the claim that you waste the firm's funds and answer like this:

"Of course I care about the company; it matters a lot to me."

Or you can use a completely impersonal response, ignoring the fact that you *personally* are being accused of waste, and answer like this:

"Nothing is more frustrating than the feeling that expenses are out of control."

Responding as in these examples instead of taking the verbal abuser's bait and running with it doesn't make you a "wimp" or a "doormat." Not at all. Putting a fire out instead of throwing gasoline on it isn't submissive or passive or cowardly. Ignoring the bait and responding neutrally to another part of the attack lets you avoid the fight and send the message that you refuse to serve as verbal victim. Furthermore, it lets you do so with no loss of face either for you or for the abuser. *This is a demonstration of your communication skills that you can be genuinely proud of.*

The Second Barrier: Guilt

When someone has always been able to rely on you to play the role of verbal victim, and you suddenly refuse to do that any longer, you're taking away something the abuser values. Many verbal abusers will then try to lay a burden of guilt on you, with a speech like this one:

"You know . . . you used to be so much <u>fun</u> to be around! I used to know, no matter <u>how</u> rotten my day had been, that I could count on <u>you</u> to brighten things <u>up</u> for me! But now . . . I don't know . . . you've CHANGED. Now, talking to you only makes me feel WORSE."

If the verbal abuser is someone you love, or someone who doesn't fit your image of an attacker—perhaps someone who's sick or very frail, for example—it's natural for you to feel guilty and slip back into the victim role. But what you must remember is this:

✦ Verbal violence is as dangerous for the abuser as for the victim.

Remember: People who are lonely and hostile are far more likely to have serious health problems. They not only face the dangers that everyone else faces in a hostile environment, they also are unlikely to have a network of supportive people who are willing to help with such things as getting to and from the doctor, remembering to take medications, and the like. Verbal abusers pay severe penalties for their habit; helping them indulge in it is much like handing a glass of wine to an alcoholic. It's not kind, or polite, or nurturing; it's actually *harmful.*

It's also important to remember that if there are children in your home your participation as victim in verbal abuser–verbal victim interactions teaches *them* that this is the way to handle conflict and disagreement. You would be helping to provide them with the "conversation as combat" model; that's not something you want to do.

You can set your feeling of guilt firmly aside, therefore, with a clear conscience. And when the abuser complains that losing you as the victim half of a verbal violence tango is painful—which is sure to be true—you need only say, with equal honesty, "I'm sorry to hear that." It's all right to regret the fact that the verbal abuser finds the change uncomfortable, but you have *no* reason to feel guilty.

If You're a Verbal Abuser

For verbal abusers the problem of following through is a matter of *resisting temptation,* just like resisting a temptation to smoke or drink or overeat or gamble. The sensation of power and satisfaction you get when you try a verbal attack and it succeeds is *pleasure*. No human being likes to give up behavior that can be relied on to provide pleasure, especially when getting it has become a habit.

It would be nice to think that you could just make up your mind not to do verbal abuse and — because of the strength of your character and will — that would be enough. If that's true of you, you're an unusual person and should be congratulated. For most human beings in the real world, however, it's *not* enough. We go right on doing things we know we should not do, even when we genuinely want to stop doing them.

Until you've had some experience with the pleasure that comes from *good* communication, giving up verbal abuse is likely to be a struggle for you. Reviewing the facts about the dangers of indulging in verbal abuse, one more time, will help.

• For all illnesses and injuries, across the board, the most important risk factors are loneliness and exposure to chronic hostility.

• Hostility and loneliness are tied together, because nobody wants to be around hostile people. Being hostile *guarantees* loneliness, over time.

• People who are hostile get sick and injured more often; it takes them longer to recover; they suffer more complications during recovery; and they die sooner.

• People who provide verbally abusive models to their children are likely to have verbally abusive *grand*children to deal with down the road. (Not to mention the consequences, both social and financial, of having adult children who don't communicate successfully with others.)

That is: *It's in your own self-interest to stop participating in verbal abuse.* If you can do it for philosophical reasons, because you understand that it's a better way to go, that's admirable; if you can do it for the sake of other people around you, that's wonderful. But suppose you *can't*. Suppose that, because you're human, philosophical reasons and altruistic reasons aren't enough to outweigh the satisfaction you get from verbal abuse. In that case, give it up for your own *self*. Do it for what's in it for *you*!

If you're thinking that the facts about the dangers of smoking or taking drugs and the benefits of quitting don't seem to help people give up their habits, you're right. It happens that most temptations we human beings struggle with . . . like cigarettes or alcohol or sex or junk food or gambling . . . *are* harder to resist, for the very simple reason that we can give in to those temptations all by ourselves. It may be a lot less fun to do alone, but it's at least possible.

✦ Verbal abuse is different. You can't do it alone; you have to have a participating partner. The satisfaction isn't in your own language, the way it would be in your own smoking or drinking or eating. *The satisfaction is in the reaction — the attentive and emotional words and body language — of your victim.*

You can't get that reaction, and the satisfaction that comes from it, by shouting abuse into the wind or at a potted plant. As I've said before, this is a situation where it really *does* take two to tango. Be glad it's that way; you're *lucky* it's that way! Because that fact — plus your knowledge that giving up verbal abuse also brings you the benefits of better health — will help you follow through.

If your situation allows you to, ask the person (or persons) you rely on for verbal victim service to be your partners in kicking the verbal abuse habit. Have them read this book so that they will understand how they can help.

And when you give in and fall back on verbal abuse, don't torment yourself about it. Tell the person you abused that you are genuinely sorry, and then set the guilt aside and try again. Every time you succeed, every time you carry on positive communication with another person instead of abusive communication, it will get easier. You will discover that good communication is *also* pleasure and that there is good feeling in abundance that comes from being someone whose company other people would enjoy. Failure is natural; failure is human. The only failure that anyone should be ashamed of is failing to *try*.

If You're an Involved Bystander

If your way of dealing with others' verbal abuse in your presence is simply to sit in misery waiting for it to be over, your choices are clear. Give it some very careful thought: *Do you really have to stay and listen?* If you're a child, you probably do. If you would get fired for refusing to stay, and that would be disastrous for you, you probably do. Otherwise, please consider your options. Sit down and complete this statement:

"If I leave when _____ and _____

start one of their confrontations, the worst thing that can

happen is _____

_____."

If your answer is that someone "wouldn't like it" or "would think I was rude" or "would think I was criticizing," if your answer is that you would be embarrassed or feel awkward — even if your answer is that one or the other of the parties would complain later about your leaving — then *leave*. Just stand up and say, "Excuse me — I've got to be going" or whatever is appropriate at the time. You don't have to stay, and you *shouldn't* stay. Your presence, even when you're not taking part in any direct way, transmits a message that you're not opposed to what's going on.

Suppose your answer is more serious — for example, "If I leave when Mom and Dad start one of their confrontations, they'll keep on until somebody really gets *hurt*." In that case, and in any situation where your feeling is that you have to stay on someone else's behalf, consider these questions: Can you actually stay and *help*? Can you stay and clearly register your opposition? By staying, can you make the others *stop* the verbal abuse?

Most of the time, the answer to these questions is no. Suppose your rank relative to the abuser and victim allows you to speak out and express your objections to the ongoing verbal violence in no uncertain terms. One of the following three things is likely to happen:

- The victim will turn on you and tell you to mind your own business, often defending the abuser with statements like "He doesn't really <u>mean</u> the things he's saying, you know!" or "She's just up<u>set</u>; she's not really like this at <u>all</u>!"

- The abuser will be delighted, because now there's <u>another</u> person participating and providing the desired feedback.

- The abuse will stop — for that moment. But at the first opportunity the abuser will use your interference as an excuse to start a new episode of abuse, taking it out on the victim you were trying to help.

The only reliably helpful thing you can do for either abuser or victim is *to make it possible for them to learn how to deal with the problem themselves*. Anything else you do, 99 times out of 100, will only tie you into the role of either Participant or Witness. All over this country, for example, there are adults who sit silently witnessing verbal abuse between their parents, with the idea that being there will keep the abuser from "going too far." They may be right, but they are making themselves part of the problem. A troupe composed of Verbal Abuser, Verbal Victim, and Disapproving Witness is just a variation on the basic verbal abuser–verbal victim pair; it's not a solution.

What to Do about It:
Dealing with English Verbal Attack Patterns

You might think that verbal abuse would be endlessly varied, with everyone who uses it thinking of newer and more ingenious ways to go about it. It's not like that. There is in fact a small set of patterns — the verbal attack patterns (VAPs, for short) — that probably account for at least half of all verbal abuse all by themselves. The example on page 130, "If you REALLY loved me, YOU wouldn't waste MONEY the way you do!", is one of those patterns. They're toxic waste; you don't want them around. For both verbal abusers and verbal victims, simply getting the VAPs out of your language environment will bring about a significant improvement. Here are some examples from the set, with a suggested response.

1. "If you REALLY cared about your health, YOU wouldn't SPEND your whole day watching television!"

    (Also appears as "If you really CARED about your health . . ." and "A person who REALLY cares . . ." or "who really CARES . . .")

    The bait here—the open attack—is "You spend your whole day watching television." This is the part of the attack that the verbal abuser expects you to notice and get upset about. Ignore it and respond to the *presupposed* attack in "If you REALLY cared about your health" instead. It presupposes that you don't care about your health; respond to that presupposition, like this:

    "Of course I care about my health."

2. "If you REALLY cared anything about your family, YOU wouldn't WANT to smoke three packs of cigarettes a day!"

Bait: "You smoke three packs of cigarettes a day."

Response: "When did you start thinking I don't care about my family?" (Responding to the presupposed "You don't care about your family.")

—or—

    "The idea that people can control their desires by will power alone is an interesting concept." (Responding to the presupposed "You could voluntarily keep from wanting to smoke three packs of cigarettes a day, if you only would.")

3. "You could at LEAST call your MOTHer once in a while!"

Bait: "You never call your mother."

Response: "You're absolutely right. People like to get phone calls from their kids." (Responding to the presupposed "Calling one's mother occasionally is the absolute minimum effort decency dictates.")

4. "WHY do you eat SO MUCH JUNK food?"

Bait: "You eat too much junk food—you're always eating junk food."

Response: "I read an article on that subject only the other day, in *Newsweek*. No, wait a minute! It wasn't *Newsweek*; it must have been the *Atlantic Monthly*, because . . ." (etc.; a Boring Baroque Response to the presupposed "You know the answer to this question and I'm asking you to share it with me.")

5. "YOU'RE not the ONly person with PROBlems, you know!"

Bait: "You think your problems are more important than anybody else's problems; you think your problems should get <u>all</u> the attention."

Response: "You're absolutely right." (Responding to the presupposed "Other people besides you have problems," which is unquestionably a true statement.)

6. "EVen somebody YOUR age should be able to balance a CHECKbook!"

Bait: "You can't balance a checkbook" and "Your age is a bad feature—you're too old." (Or too young.)

Response: "The idea that people my age are somehow inferior is something you hear now and then; I'm astonished to hear it from <u>you</u>." (Or "I'm sorry you feel that way.") (Responding to the presupposed "People your age have something wrong with them just because they're your age.")

Read the six example VAPs aloud, putting heavy stress on the parts that are in capital letters, and *listen* to them. Move the stresses around a little, as in the shift from "If you REALLY cared" to "If you really CARED." Notice that you can rely on your internal grammar: You'll know exactly which changes are and aren't possible.

There are more patterns in the set of VAPs, though not very many more. For all of them, the same basic technique applies:

- Ignore the bait.

- Respond to something that is presupposed.

- Whatever else you do, transmit this message: "I won't serve as verbal victim for you; I don't play that game."

Remember: All of us lose our temper and use these patterns once in a while; that's not the problem. We just apologize and put the episode behind us. But if you're using the patterns routinely — or helping someone else use them routinely, by taking the bait they contain and responding to it — you're polluting your language environment. This is something you can follow through on and *fix*.

Another Look at Scenario Six

Nothing that Geneva Sheridan does in the scenario takes great skill or is particularly complicated. Whenever Jerry throws out a chunk of bait, she ignores it. And each time, she responds with something that (1) won't feed the hostility loop and (2) causes no loss of face for her, for Charlotte, or for Jerry. That is: She flatly refuses to play the role of either victim or involved bystander, and she does so in a way that causes no loss of face for anyone present. Let's look at just one sequence.

Jerry: "Well, if it's not Counselor <u>She</u>ridan! Tell me . . . to <u>what</u> do we owe <u>this</u> honor?"

Geneva: "It's this porch, Jerry. No matter how hot it is, this porch always has a cool breeze. I can't resist it."

Jerry's utterance is a mildly sarcastic attempt to provoke Geneva. A cruder abuser might have put it this way:

"Well, if it's not the hotshot lady lawyer! How come you're slumming around with us?"

Jerry's more subtle than that, but that's the message he was sending, and both women understand it. Suppose Geneva had taken the bait; then we might have had this mess . . .

Jerry: "Well, if it's not Counselor Sheridan! Tell me . . . to what do we owe this honor?"

Geneva: "I'm here to see Charlotte, Jerry, not you; just chalk it up to my bad timing, okay?"

Jerry: "Hey, not to worry, Counselor! I'll just LEAVE, so you two 'professional women' can get on with your important conversation . . . that SUIT YOU?"

Charlotte: "Jerry, PLEASE don't be like that! I'm sure Geneva didn't mean to suggest that you should leave!"

Jerry: "Charlotte, your sister and I understand each other, DON'T we, Geneva? I understand BOTH of you! And I am sick and TIRED of you two females sneaking around behind my BACK like you do!"

(And so on . . . downhill all the way.)

Similarly, when Jerry attacks Charlotte openly, claiming that she always grabs the floor at the first mention of anything medical, his intention is to provoke Geneva into a defense of her sister — something Charlotte mistakenly thinks would be a good idea. But Geneva again ignores the bait, opening with, "People are very interested in the health care system." Not, "Jerry, Charlotte is very interested in the health care system," but "people" are interested. Geneva's response is free of personal language and free of extra stresses on words and parts of words. And then she turns toward Jerry, indicating that he now has the floor, and asks him for his opinion about the likelihood of nationalized health care in America.

Certainly Jerry could continue with his abuse, if he were determined to do so. For example, he could say:

"Why don't you ask your <u>sister</u> that question? SHE's the
one who considers herself an <u>ex</u>pert on the subject, not <u>me</u>!"

Some chronic verbal abusers are like this—persistent and very
determined, convinced that if they just hang in there their intended
victim will eventually give up and play the role. In such a case,
Geneva Sheridan would answer like this:

"Experts on health care are under every rock these days; it's
amazing. And it just demonstrates how very much people
<u>care</u> about the issue. They don't see it as a trivial matter."

That is: *No matter how many times Jerry comes at Geneva with
hostile language about herself or about Charlotte, Geneva will continue to deflect the abuse with impersonal and neutral language.*
This will be just as true if he switches from sarcasm to using the
VAPs—Geneva is just not going to accommodate him. It may take a
while, but eventually Jerry will realize that his plan, in which he
and Charlotte and Geneva will waste half an hour in an ugly confrontation, is never going to work. At that point, he will give it up.

Jerry can't fight all by himself; he has to have help from at least
one of the women.

✦ The more persistent verbal abusers are, the more important it is
not to give in and take the bait. Because each time you *do* give
in, it reinforces their conviction that you *will* participate if they
just stick to their guns.

Geneva has found herself, through no fault of her own, in the
middle of an attempt by a verbal abuser to set up a hostility loop
with his usual victim and involve her in the resulting scene. She
wouldn't hesitate to leave if the attempt began to work, but she's
skillful enough to prevent that, and so she stays. She is an excellent
model for Charlotte and Jerry, if they would only pay attention and
profit by her example.

Step 6 Backup

◆

Working with the English Verbal Attack Patterns

To increase your skill in recognizing and responding to verbal attack patterns, copy the VAP examples below onto a diary page in your verbal self-defense notebook. Then answer questions A, B, and C, for each one.

A. What is the bait in this attack?

B. What are the presuppositions in this attack?

C. What could someone say as an answer to this attack that would ignore the bait, respond directly to a presupposition, and send the message "I won't play that game"—all without causing a loss of face for anyone involved?

For instance . . .

VAP: "If you REALLY cared about your family, YOU wouldn't PICK on everybody all the time!"

A. **Bait:** You pick on everybody in your family all the time.

B. **Presupposition:** You don't really care about your family.

C. **Response:** "When did you start thinking that I don't care about my family?"—or—"Of course I care about my family."

◆ NOTE: Any sentence includes presuppositions that aren't relevant for this exercise. For example, the phrase "your family" has the presupposition "You have a family." You could find all of these presuppositions if you wanted to do so, because you are a native speaker of your language; but you don't need to write them all down. Just write down the ones that *are* relevant.

VAP EXAMPLES

1. "Parents who really LOVE their children don't neGLECT them!"

143

2. "DON'T you even CARE if your HAIRcut makes you look STU-PID?"

3. "DON'T you even CARE if your HAIRCUT is BREAKING your mother's HEART?"

4. "WHY is it imPOSSible for you to follow inSTRUCtions?"

5. "EVen if you DO lose your job, WE won't think you're a failure!"

6. "EVerybody underSTANDS why you don't do your share of the WORK around here, you know!"

7. "You could at LEAST TRY to get home on time!"

8. "You KNOW I'd never tell you what to DO, dear, but if you inSIST on taking that JOB, you're going to be MISerable!"

9. "SOME people would get a diVORCE if their spouses treated them like SLAVES."

10. "You're only DOing that to make me feel IGnorant!"

Verbal Attack Pattern Incident Log

Here's another page to set up in your diary. You have two goals:

1. To find out how often you (and people you interact with on a regular basis) use the verbal attack patterns.

2. To keep track of the results you observe when you respond to others' VAPs or they respond to yours.

DATE: _____

DESCRIPTION OF THE SITUATION:

A VERBAL ATTACK PATTERN I HEARD SOMEONE USE / I MYSELF USED:

WHAT WAS SAID IN RESPONSE TO THE VAP:

WHAT WAS SAID NEXT:
   (Repeat as many times as necessary to record the whole interaction.)

WHAT HAPPENED—THE CONSEQUENCES:

(And if things didn't go well . . .)
A BETTER RESPONSE TO THE VAP:

COMMENTS:

TOTAL NUMBER OF VAPS I'VE USED SO FAR THIS MONTH:

_____

TOTAL NUMBER OF VAPS I'VE HEARD FROM OTHERS SO FAR THIS MONTH: _____

✦ SIGHT BITES ✦
Quotations to Think About and Use

"Talking out an emotion doesn't reduce it, it rehearses it."

— and —

"[C]ouples who yell at each other do not thereafter feel less angry but more angry."

(Tavris 1982, p. 32.)

◆

Maintaining Your Own Healthy Language Environment

I know that a person who participates in verbal abuse is like a polluted well — a source from which trouble spreads in ever-widening circles. From now on, I refuse to be one of those sources.

———————————— Scenario Seven ————————————

Travis Brown was in a good mood. He'd made it through the tax season without having to ask even one of his clients to file for an extension; the lemon eucalyptus trees he was trying to grow for sale as houseplants were looking great; and Jerry had just phoned to report that little Adam had taken his first step. So far as Travis was concerned, all was right with his world; he sat down to eat his breakfast, ready for a terrific day . . .

And looked up from his plate to see Lydia frowning at him over the scrambled eggs.

"Something wrong, honey?" he asked her.

"You're <u>humming</u> again, Travis!" she said. "I cannot <u>stand</u> it when you <u>hum</u>!"

"Oh," he said. "I'm sorry."

"If you would at <u>least</u> try to hum a <u>tune</u>!"

"I said I was sorry, Lydia — I won't <u>hum</u>. All RIGHT?"

"Well, you don't have to SNAP at me, Travis!"

As Travis walked into his office, he could hear the phone ringing on his desk, but then it stopped.

Elaine Gordon looked up from her computer and smiled at him. "Good morning, Mr. Brown," she said.

"Why doesn't anybody ever answer the <u>phone</u> around here?" Travis demanded. "Are you all DEAF?"

"Sorry, sir," Elaine answered. "We're not open yet — I didn't think you'd want it answered."

She was right, and Travis knew it; but he went straight on to his desk without another word.

Ten minutes later, the UPS man arrived with the morning deliveries. "Morning!" he said, smiling over his armload of mailing envelopes and boxes.

"It's about TIME you got here!" Ellen snapped. She snatched the clipboard out of his hand, scribbled her signature on the papers, and handed it all back, the scowl on her face just daring him to object.

He was used to this kind of thing, and he had better things to do with his time than argue with secretaries who had inflated impressions of their own importance. He took the clipboard, jerked his head at her, turned on his heel, and left. When he made his next delivery, he was careful not to smile.

◆

What's Going On Here?

Everybody's Point of View

All the people in Scenario Seven would claim that they were just going about their business, bothering nobody, when one of the others came along and spoiled everything.

Lydia was feeling fine and was expecting a pleasant breakfast with her husband — until he sat down and started that maddening *hum*ming that he knows she *hates.*

Travis was ready for a wonderful day, absolutely delighted with it — until Lydia chewed him out for *hum*ming, as if he'd robbed a *bank.*

Ellen was contentedly at work on a project she enjoyed — until

Travis walked in and gave her a hard time about answering a telephone that he *knew* she wasn't *supposed* to answer.

The UPS delivery man had expected it to be a good day, and was looking forward to it—until Ellen took his *head* off for being three minutes later than *suited* her. And he won't knock himself out being pleasant to the next person he has to deal with; why go *looking* for trouble?

In this scenario, Lydia would claim that Travis started the chain of hostile language with his dadblasted *humming*, and Travis would say that Lydia started it with her ridiculous *complaining* . . . and so it would go, right on down the line. The point of view of each person involved can be stated this way:

"I was <u>fine</u> until <u>you</u> ruined my DAY!"

It will go on like this in an endless chain, with the hostility passing from person to person like salmonella bacteria. Unless some exceedingly nice things happen during the day—nice enough to outweigh the entire accumulation of negative emotions—everyone in the chain will go to bed thinking what a rotten world we live in, and how full it is of *weird people*, all of them out to get you! Which proves that—

Language Behavior Is Contagious

The image of the speaker as a polluted well is an ugly metaphor, and a painful one. We know from long experience that it's accurate—we've all been through days like the one presented in Scenario Seven—but it's not easy to face. However, when we consider it scientifically rather than emotionally, the picture is a great deal brighter. *Because the same natural laws that make the contaminated well a threat make the* wholesome *one a blessing.* We can just as easily be the source of good feeling as of bad; it's our choice.

Suppose you arrive at your office in a bad mood, and one of your colleagues comes over and tells you something that you feel makes no sense at all. Suppose you immediately apply Miller's-Law-In-Reverse. You assume that what you heard was false; you wonder what's wrong with your colleague to account for it having been said; and you react accordingly. The colleague feels your negative reaction and comes away from the encounter feeling put down. When he then talks to someone else in the office, *he* sounds hostile, and that annoys his listener, who answers him with hostility in *her* voice and goes away in a bad mood too. *All day long, people will pass along these negative feelings* — the ones that started with *you*. Hostility spreads from the source and is passed along by language, from mild unpleasantness to overt verbal violence.

However, this is a cloud with a golden lining, because pleasant and positive language behavior functions in exactly the same way. People who talk to us and come away feeling that they were not just heard, but actually *listened* to, feel better. Even if they don't think we really understood what they said . . . even if they know we disagreed with what they said . . . they feel better. The fact that we were willing to listen and make an effort to understand makes them feel more positive, and this feeling is then reflected in their language.

It's one of the enduring miracles of human communication that in the same way that the effects of language spread from one person to another when they're negative, they spread when they are positive as well. As a result, the techniques and strategies in this eight-step program work *even when nobody else knows you're using them.* They even work when used around people who, if asked, would insist that they *couldn't* work.

It's very important to understand that this does *not* mean we have to tailor our language behavior in ways that misrepresent our feelings. It doesn't mean we can't use negative words when they are necessary and appropriate. There will be many times when we must say no, when we must refuse, when we must offer criticism or complaint, when we must report unpleasant facts, and when we must disagree.

However, it *does* mean that we have both an opportunity and a responsibility. *Because we have the linguistic resources to do all those negative things in a* nondestructive way, *without adding extra messages of hostility and anger and abuse.* And we have the linguistic resources to establish and maintain a language environment in which we also have many opportunities to say *yes* . . . opportunies to accept, to offer praise rather than criticism, to report facts that cause pleasure rather than pain, and to agree with others.

In the April 1993 issue of *Reason,* Jonathan Rauch made the astonishing claim that *science itself* is in grave danger if we accept the idea that "hurtful words are a form of violence." Of the principle that it's wrong to hurt others with words he wrote: "This principle is a menace—and not just to civil liberties. At bottom it threatens liberal inquiry—that is, science itself."

Suppose it were true that messages containing negative *facts*— such as the news that someone has failed an exam, that someone's research results have been proved wrong, that someone's grant proposal is not going to be funded—could only be transmitted in a negative *manner*. Then Rauch would be right. For the sake of scientific inquiry, we would have to accept verbal abuse with the same resigned regret we reserve for hurricanes and earthquakes and other "acts of God." We can all be very glad that it's *not* true, and that human language is far richer and more flexible than Rauch realizes.

What to Do about It: Using the Satir Modes

You know how to recognize language that everyone will acknowledge to be hostile, and you know some practical techniques for dealing with openly abusive language effectively. Now we want to examine some abusive language that may be a bit harder to identify, and discuss a method for avoiding it ourselves and defusing it when it comes at us from others.

Suppose a woman is asked by her son and daughter-in-law if she will stay with their two children while they go out to dinner to celebrate a promotion. She might answer like this:

> "WHY do you two ALWAYS try to take ADVANTAGE of me? It NEVER OCCURS to you that I MIGHT have plans of my OWN, DOES it? I certainly will NOT stay with your kids!"

We would all agree: That's hostile! That's verbal abuse, going far beyond what we needed for a simple refusal. She could have transmitted the message that she wouldn't babysit by simply saying, "Sorry, I already have plans; I can't do it this time." The hostile speech above adds many extra messages, all of them unpleasant, to that basic content. But there is still another way the mother-in-law could have answered. Like this:

> "Well, of COURSE I'll stay with the kids! YOU know how I am ... ANYTHING I can DO to HELP, I'm HAPPY to do it! You two just RUN along and enJOY yourselves, and don't even THINK about ME — I never mind being left out, dears, YOU know that. I'll just MAKE do with whatEVER LEFTOVERS you HAVE in the fridge ..."

Notice: The *words* themselves are sweetness and light. There isn't a single word of open abuse in the whole long utterance. But every native speaker of English understands that this woman not only isn't going to stay with her grandchildren, she is also determined to ruin the couple's evening. *Whether they go out and leave her with their kids or not, the occasion will be spoiled.* And if they object, she will be able to say with false astonishment, "But I don't underSTAND! I TOLD you — I'd LOVE to babysit for you!"

The two possible replies to the babysitting request seem very different at first glance and first hearing, but they're *both* verbal abuse. They both will spread negative feeling, and equally well. They are examples of two different communication styles that people use in situations of possible conflict.

The openly hostile style is called *Blaming*; the falsely pleasant one is called *Placating*. (The terms come from Virginia Satir, who was the first to isolate and describe the patterns in each style.) When we use Blaming language, almost everyone will agree that we're being verbally abusive. If we're Placating, however, it's often possible to convince ourselves (and others) that our speech is *not* verbal abuse.

To end this confusion, we need to compare the two styles carefully. Although they seem different on the surface, they have in common the two primary identifying features of all hostile language:

- Frequent stresses on words and parts of words — stresses that are not needed to convey contrast or surprise.

- Frequent use of very personal language — especially the set of personal pronouns ("I/me/my/mine/we/us/our/ours/you/your/ yours/myself/yourself/ourselves/yourselves").

In addition, these two modes will often include facial expressions, gestures, and postures that help the speakers express their negative emotional messages.

Blaming and Placating spread hostility, no matter how "nice" the words might look if they were written down without any information about intonation. Remember Pollyanna? Pollyanna, caught in a hurricane, would say, "Oh, I just <u>love</u> a nice <u>wind</u>, don't <u>you</u>?" And we would all want to throw her out a window and watch her blow away. But "all she said was" that she enjoys a nice wind and wonders if we share that feeling!

✦ The *emotional* messages we send, whether positive or negative, are carried not by the words we say but by the way we say them. Those messages are carried by our body language, while "All I <u>said</u> was . . ." always refers only to our words. It's almost *never* a valid excuse.

In addition to Blaming and Placating, Dr. Satir identified three other patterns typical of language people use when they are are tense and under stress: *Computing, Distracting,* and *Leveling.* The skillful use — (or skillful avoidance) of these Satir Modes — is one of the most powerful techniques available to us for establishing and maintaining positive rather than negative communication. Let's examine them further.

Computing is very different from Blaming and Placating. It uses only those items of personal language that the speaker really cannot avoid, and relies heavy on abstractions, generalizations, generic, and hypothetical references, and the like. On page 113, when Lee responds to Tracy's accusation by remarking that people find it irritating when their belongings aren't where they ought to be, Lee's response is in Computer Mode. Computing *intonation* is neutral, without the extra stresses on words and parts of words that are typical of Blaming and Placating, and the rest of the body language used is neutral also.

Distracting *combines* the other modes, with a sentence or two from one style, then a sentence or two from another, cycling through the modes with the body language shifting right along with the words. This is the language of *panic*. We can summarize its message as: "HELP! I don't know what to SAY!"

That leaves Leveling, which can be recognized by the fact that *it has none of the identifying features of the other four Satir Modes*. Leveling is the simple truth, spoken in order to *communicate* that truth, without extra messages and agendas laid on. Theoretically, Leveling is perfect communication; in the real world, however, it is not always appropriate or safe. Suppose your boss calls you in and says, neutrally, "You don't like me, do you?" and you answer, neutrally, "You're right. I can't stand the sight of you." That's Leveling, and in the scientific sense it's a flawless exchange of truthful messages — but it could get you fired, with serious consequences for you and those who depend on you.

You already know these patterns (although you may not have known their names). They are part of your internal grammar. The easiest way to make them clear is to imagine five people, one from each mode, in a single stressful situation. Suppose they are all sitting in a waiting room at a medical clinic, and they've all had to wait long past the time of their appointment with a doctor. Suppose no one has had the courtesy to offer them an explanation of any kind. Here's what they might say:

Blaming: "WHY IS it that EVERY time I COME here I have to sit and WAIT for HOURS?? MY time is valuable TOO, you know!"

Placating: "I just KNOW the doctors have a good REASON for being so LATE! And I REALLY don't MIND being kept waiting like this . . . I mean, I don't have anything BETter to do, ANYway!"

Computing: "Everybody hates it when doctors keep them waiting; an explanation would be helpful."

Distracting: "WHY can't that doctor EVer keep her APPOINTments on time? It's disGRACEful to have to sit and WAIT like this! Not that I had anything important to DO, of course . . . you know ME . . . There is undoubtedly a good reason for the delay;

no sensible person would be angry. But I am SICK and TIRED of WAITing!"

Leveling: "My appointment was at two o'clock, and it's three-twenty now. This is inexcusable; I'm going home."

You recognize the Satir Modes automatically; you can rely on your internal grammar for that. The question is, how do you *respond* to them in a way that keeps hostility to a minimum? Easy! You use the familiar basic metaprinciple: ANYTHING YOU FEED WILL GROW. Setting up a loop based on any Satir Mode and feeding it at both ends—for example, responding to Blaming language by Blaming back—will cause that behavior to escalate. Setting up a loop based on hostile language—for example, responding to Blaming language by Placating, or vice versa—will create more and more hostility.

This is just as true when one of the people involved is a child as when both are adults; children learn their Satir Mode strategies from observing their parents and other adults (or older children) in their language environment. We have all seen dialogues like this one, in which the mother tries to handle the child's Blaming by answering in Placater Mode . . .

Child: "I don't WANT that old cereal! I WANT the ONE with MARSHmallows in it!"

Mother: "Oh, honey, PLEASE don't start acting like that! Tell you what—YOU and I will make a DEAL, oKAY?? YOU be a GOOD girl while we get the rest of the GROCeries, and THEN we'll go get some ICE cream! OKAY?"

Child: "NO! I don't WANT ice cream! I want you to get me the CEReal with MARSHmallows in it!"

Mother: "But, HONey . . ."

No child should be able to pull an adult's linguistic strings in this fashion. But interactions like this one, and a multitude of variations on the same theme, can be seen and heard everywhere you go. Children don't make these patterns *up*; they learn them by observation.

You might want to keep that in mind when you're tempted to feed a hostility loop by Blaming or Placating; it will help you resist the temptation.

In this case there's no need to set up separate strategies for verbal abusers, verbal victims, and involved bystanders. Where the Satir Modes are concerned, the rule is the same for everyone:

✦   No Blaming; No Placating; No Distracting.

You create and maintain a nonhostile language environment, whether the facts contained in your message are positive or negative in their content, by choosing between Leveling and Computing. You base your choice on your knowledge of the real-world situation, your knowledge of the grammar, and your communication goals.

Suppose your elderly mother appears in a new green dress and asks you for your opinion. Suppose the dress isn't flattering, and your honest opinion is that she looks terrible. What do you say, if your goal is to avoid hostility?

Here are three Leveling choices:

1. "That dress doesn't flatter you, Mother; you don't look good at all."

2. "I like that shade of green very much, Mother."

3. "I don't like that shade of green very much, Mother."

And here are three Computing choices, with all personal language carefully avoided:

4. "Judging another person's appearance isn't easy, Mother; different people have different tastes."

5. "Green is a very nice color, Mother."

6. "Green can be a tricky color to wear, Mother."

If you have a good — and nonhostile — reason to use #1, do so. It's the truth, and there are situations when it might have to be said.

Otherwise, don't say it. The other two Leveling responses may be better choices, because they comment on the dress rather than on your mother's appearance. The Computing responses are safer still, especially if you already know (or can tell from body language) that your mother is feeling depressed or insecure, or that she's nervous about her appearance. None of these six responses requires you to lie or causes anyone to lose face. Compare them, please, with the responses below:

Blaming:

"You're NOT going to wear THAT, are YOU?"

"EVen a woman YOUR age should have SOME clothes sense!"

"How could you POSSibly have bought anything in that HOR-RIBLE COLor?"

"That's the UGliest dress I ever SAW!"

"Perhaps it would be better, Mother, if you let ME pick out something for you NEXT time."

"Mother, you KNOW you look awful in green!"

Placating:

"GOODness, WHY are you asking ME? I mean, I don't know anything about women's CLOTHES . . ."

"Oh, YOU know ME, Mother — no matter WHAT you wear, I'LL always think you look beautiful!"

All of these utterances are hostile and abusive, and not one is excusable.

Let's look again at an exchange or two between Jerry Brown and his sister-in-law Geneva Sheridan, from Scenario Six, to illustrate how the Satir Modes were used there. The conversation was not relaxed and comfortable, remember. Jerry opened it with an attempt to provoke Geneva into a confrontation; Charlotte was tense because she expected Jerry to do precisely what he did; and Geneva was wary because she'd been present during many altercations involving Jerry and either Charlotte or someone else. Here are the lines . . .

Jerry: "I thought it was my <u>charm</u> that dragged you out of the courtroom, Geneva! I'm <u>hurt</u>."

Geneva: "Lawyers are immune to charm. Fortunately. It's a course they take in law school — Immunity 101."

Notice what happened here. Jerry is doing what men typically refer to as "only teasing." He uses lots of "I/you" personal language and two emphatic stresses (on "charm" and "hurt") that aren't required by any rules except those of the grammar of verbal violence. His utterance is an example of mild Blaming. Geneva could have answered in the same mode, saying "I'm <u>immune</u> to your charm, Jerry! <u>Fortunately</u>! It's a course I took in <u>law</u> school — Immunity one-oh-ONE!" That response would have given Jerry an excuse to go on with his attempt to provoke her. *She didn't do that.* She switched to Computer Mode and told him that "lawyers" are immune to "charm." Not that she, the lawyer, is immune to *his* charm . . . just that generic lawyers are immune to generic charm. And that lawyers, generic again, take a course in immunity to charm in law school.

Later in the conversation, when Jerry and Charlotte have just started fighting and he has attacked his wife indirectly, Geneva again defuses the confrontation with a switch to Computer Mode. Here are the lines:

Jerry: "I'm sorry, Geneva — you might as well forget about finishing your story. You can't say <u>two</u> <u>words</u> about anything <u>medical</u> around here without Nurse Charlotte grabbing the <u>floor</u>."

Geneva: "People are very interested in the health care system. It's not like contract law, or a boundary squabble. It's part of everybody's life . . ." (Etc.)

Once again Jerry has tried strongly personal language filled with extra stresses on words and parts of words, plus the sarcastic "Nurse Charlotte" and an open accusation about her behavior. And once again, Geneva refuses to take the bait and answers in Computer Mode, with statements about "people" and "everybody."

If Jerry actually *were* a mean and sadistic man, he could certainly go on with his verbal abuse. In the exchange just quoted, he could have come back at Geneva with something like this:

"WHY do you always DO THAT? I'm TALKing about your SISter here, not about 'people'! And YOU, as usual, are trying to change the SUBject! You don't have any guts at ALL, DO you, Geneva?"

If that happened, Geneva would then have to decide between Leveling and Computing as a response. Like this:

Leveling: "I have guts enough to leave when you're using me as a prop in a fight, Jerry. Good-bye!" (And she leaves, immediately.)

Computing: "People who find themselves in the middle of others' fights have only one appropriate response, and that is to leave. Good-bye." (And she leaves, immediately.)

But Jerry isn't that sort of verbal abuser—most people aren't. Geneva's replies in Computer Mode are enough to deflect his attack and put an end to the hostility. This doesn't require a major effort on Geneva's part, you'll notice, nor does she have to compromise her principles in any way. She just refuses to feed the hostility loops Jerry keeps trying to set up.

✦ Language is the most powerful tool we have for bringing about change and for creating the kind of life we want to live. It is the highest of technologies, available to every one of us in abundance and for *free*; it's part of our birthright as human beings. Skillful use of the Satir Modes is one of the most reliable and efficient methods for making good use of that technology.

Another Look at Scenario Seven

Ideally, Lydia Brown would not have tackled Travis about his hum-ming in the first place. She would have realized that the matter was trivial; for example, she would have found it impossible to con-struct a three-part message about it. "When you hum, I feel dis-tressed, because . . . ?" She couldn't have found a single concrete real-world result of Travis's humming to fill part 3 of her complaint. Ideally she would have realized that he couldn't talk and hum at the same time, and that starting a conversation would put an end to the behavior she finds so annoying.

However, let's assume that Lydia didn't use her common sense; let's assume that she went right ahead and announced, "I cannot stand it when you hum!" What could Travis have done then to pre-serve his good mood and avoid joining in the daylong chain of hos-tile language shown in the scenario?

Similarly, what could the secretary or the UPS man have done to cut off the flow of toxic language? Here are some possible rewrites at each point in the scenario where the hostility was trans-ferred from one person to another, to demonstrate that the commu-nication problems could easily have been avoided.

1. **Lydia:**   "I cannot stand it when you hum!"

   Travis: "It's hard to put up with other people's bad habits, especially early in the morning. Many a marriage faces that problem." (Computing)

   — or —

   "And I cannot help humming, Lydia, not when I feel this good. I'm afraid you'll have to either make me miserable or put up with the humming." (Leveling)

2. **Travis:**   "Why doesn't anybody ever answer the phone around here? Are you all DEAF?"

   Elaine: "You must have had a bad morning already, Mr. Brown; maybe things will go better from here on." (Leveling)

   — or —

"Answering the phones before nine o'clock is against the rules." (Computing)

— or —

"As you know, Mr. Brown, answering the phones before we're open for business is against the rules." (Leveling)

3. **Elaine:** "It's about TIME you got here!"

   UPS Man: "Hey — I'm three minutes late. Long enough to cook a softboiled egg. Not long enough to throw a company into a tailspin." (Leveling)

   — or —

   "When a day starts out badly, even the little things seem like too much to bear." (Computing)

In each of these examples, the hostility chain has been broken off by the proper choice of Satir Modes. Not by a choice of better *words*, however. Look at the examples below.

Travis: "I cannot HELP humming, Lydia, not when I feel THIS good! I'm afraid you'll have to either MAKE me MISerable or PUT UP with the humming!"

Elaine: "ANswering the PHONES before nine o'CLOCK is against the RULES!"

UPS Man: "HEY — I'm THREE MINUTES LATE! LONG enough to do a soft-boiled EGG! NOT long enough to throw a company into a TAILspin!"

Same words — very different melodies. And it's the melodies that count . . . .

Step 7 Backup

---◆---

Satir Mode Log

The purpose of this diary page is to help you keep track of language interactions where you can clearly see (and hear and feel) the effect of the Satir Mode choices that are made—by you yourself, or by others. Record the language in as much detail as you can, being sure to include body language that you observed at the time.

DATE: _____

DESCRIPTION OF THE SITUATION:

THE UTTERANCE IN _____ MODE (BLAMING, PLACATING, COMPUTING, DISTRACTING, OR LEVELING) THAT STARTED THE INTERACTION:

THE RESPONSE IN _____ MODE THAT FOL-LOWED:

WHAT THE FIRST SPEAKER SAID NEXT:

WHAT THE SECOND SPEAKER SAID NEXT:

(Repeat as many times as necessary to record the whole interaction.)

WHAT HAPPENED—THE CONSEQUENCES:

COMMENTS:

Personal Satir Mode Incident Log

DATE: _____

DESCRIPTION OF THE SITUATION:

UTTERANCE IN _____ MODE THAT I HEARD SOMEONE USE / THAT I MYSELF USED:

RESPONSE IN _____ MODE:

WHAT THE FIRST SPEAKER SAID NEXT:

WHAT THE SECOND SPEAKER SAID NEXT:

(Repeat as many times as necessary to record the whole interaction.)

WHAT HAPPENED—THE CONSEQUENCES:

COMMENTS:

More on Using the Satir Modes

1. You'll remember from the discussion of the sensory modes (in Step 4) that people have a strong preference for one of those modes over the others, especially when they are tense or under stress. The same thing is true for the Satir Modes: People under stress tend to rely on the Satir Mode that they feel works best for them.

   However, there's an important difference. *Although a person's preferred sensory mode will be the same in every situation, this is not true of the Satir Mode preference.* Some people rely on Blaming to handle tense situations at work but prefer Placating when they have to deal with similar situations at home, and vice versa. Many people always Placate with doctors but usually use Blamer Mode with nurses.

   Start keeping track of your own Satir Mode preferences and habits. Which of the modes do you tend to fall back on in which situations?

2. It's also useful to know which Satir Mode is preferred by people you spend a lot of time with. Observe the language behavior of your spouse—your children—your boss or employee—your close friends—when they're not just carrying on casual relaxed conversations. Which Satir Mode does each one rely on most when tense? In which situations? Set up a record of this information in your diary, so that you'll have it when you are anticipating stressful communication with any of these individuals.

3. Remembering that translation is *finding the utterance that would have been used by a speaker of the other language or variety of language in the same situation,* collect examples of Satir Mode utterances, write them on a diary page, and translate them into *different* Satir Modes. It's especially useful to get a lot of practice translating Blaming or Placating utterances into Computer Mode, which—unlike Leveling—doesn't come naturally to most of us. Here is an example to get you started.

a. "It's not MY fault that our prices are so high! I only WORK here—I DON'T set the doctor's FEES!" (Blamer Mode)

b. "People forget sometimes that doctors' receptionists don't set their fees." (Computer Mode)

4. Now that you're familiar with the Satir Modes, go back and take another look at the examples of unacceptable complaints when the tomato plants are not watered, on page 70, and the list of things Charlotte would have been advised *not* to say, on page 72. For each utterance, identify its Satir Mode and fix it by translating it into a different and more useful one.

Converting Negatives to Positives

In the Sight Bites section on page 122, Renkema points out that there are an infinite number of different ways to say almost any message. Using the Satir Modes, other techniques you've learned in this program, and your own language skill, rewrite each of the negative utterances below as a positive and nonhostile version of the same message.

1. "You gave wrong answers to four of the ten questions on this exam."

2. "You only have twenty minutes to get all this work done!"

3. "I don't think you're cut out to be a historian; you'd be a lot better off in chemistry or biology."

4. "People who love other people don't go out of their way to make them miserable."

5. "It will be at least five years before you get promoted."

6. "Your proposed solution to this problem has a number of serious flaws, and only one really good suggestion."

7. "Only somebody who is both ignorant and stubborn could make a mistake like you made."

8. "If you don't start doing your homework, you're going to turn out like your Uncle <u>Charlie</u>, you <u>know</u> <u>that</u>?"

9. "Get that stupid look off your face!"

10. "I <u>knew</u> you were going to lose that job—and I was <u>right</u>! <u>Wasn't</u> I?"

✦ NOTE: Now set up a diary page in your verbal self-defense notebook and begin collecting negative utterances — your own or other people's — and converting them into positive versions in the same way as you did for the examples above. Pay attention to the way the body language used with each version would change; say each version aloud and decide what sort of facial expression, gestures, body position, and the like, you would use with that utterance.

✦ SIGHT BITES ✦
Quotations to Think About and Use

"Morale comes down from the sky like rain. If you're the boss and you're feeling lousy, watch out — you're like the plague going around!"

> (S. Leonard, Sr., quoted in "Beyond Positive Thinking," p. 34.)

"Suppose your doctor told you this after a biopsy: 'The chance that you will survive the next six months is only half.' And compare it with 'There is a fifty percent chance you will live more than six months.'"

> (Ornstein and Sobel 1987, p. 109. The authors go on to note that the first message is "a fifty percent chance of dying" while the second is "a fifty percent chance of living.")

◆

Taking Responsibility for Your Own Language—And Its Consequences

I know that I am responsible for the consequences of my language behavior. I know that language has the same potential to help or harm as the most powerful medicine or the sharpest surgical instrument. I would not use penicillin or a scalpel carelessly; I will not use language carelessly.

Scenario Eight

Charlotte was heartsick, and Jerry looked as if he felt much the same way. They had been planning the dinner—for just the two of them and Jerry's boss and his wife—for weeks; it had mattered a lot to both of them. But somehow, even though they had both wanted very much to make a good impression on Tim and Tina Hendryx, it hadn't turned out that way. Instead, they had spent the evening in almost the same kind of bickering and sulking that went on when they were alone. It had been obvious that the Hendryxes were uncomfortable, and they had left as soon after dinner as they possibly could. Now Charlotte and Jerry sat at the kitchen table, both stunned by what had happened.

"Jerry," Charlotte said, her voice trembling, "how could you?"

"How could I what?"

"YOU know what!"

"No, I <u>don't</u>, Charlotte! Spell it OUT for me!"

"You know how important that dinner was, to both of us . . . you know how <u>hard</u> I've worked getting ready for — "

"Oh, THERE we go!" Jerry cut in. "POOR Charlotte! WORK-ING her little FINGERS TO THE bone! Can't you do even ONE simple TASK without making a federal CASE OUT OF IT?"

"Jerry, don't try to change the subject! Please . . . I really want to talk about this."

"You do? You really want to TALK about the way you dis-GRACED me in front of my BOSS and his WIFE? Fine, Charlotte! Go ahead — TALK!"

"Jerry, that's not FAIR! YOU were the one who STARTED it, every single TIME!"

"Oh, YEAH? How about the time that all I said was 'Charlotte, these potatoes are so good that I'm amazed,' and YOU came back at ME with — "

"That's NOT the way you SAID it, Jerry!"

"Oh, come ON, Charlotte! How about taking a little responsibility for your own beHAVIOR for once! I said the potatoes were terrific, THAT'S all! But YOU acted like — "

"Jerry, I'M not the one that won't accept responsibility for the messes I make! THAT'S YOUR trick! You ALways try to shove ALL the blame on ME! When you said that about the potatoes, you were being sarCAStic, and YOU KNOW it!"

"I was NOT! I was COMPlimenting you! YOU'RE just too neu-rotic to RECOGNIZE a COMpliment — that's YOUR problem!"

(And so on. Getting uglier all the time.)

✦

What's Going On Here?

Charlotte's and Jerry's Point of View

Charlotte is terribly upset. She had done everything she could to set the stage for a lovely evening so that Jerry's boss and his wife would have a pleasant time and take away a lasting positive impres-sion of the Brown family. It seems to her that Jerry went out of his way to make this impossible and to make the evening a disaster for everyone present. She knows he will try to blame *her*, but she's not going to let him do it. It seems to her that the least he could do is apologize to her and admit that it was all his fault.

Jerry feels exactly the same way—except that his perception is that it's Charlotte who will try to blame *him*, and he feels that the least she could do is apologize to him and admit that it was all *her* fault.

◆

Charlotte and Jerry will sit at the kitchen table now and take the evening's language apart line by line, each trying to make a solid case against the other. With every utterance they exchange, their emotions will grow stronger, because they are vigorously feeding the hostility loop they've set up and it will escalate out of control. Each one is determined that there must be a clear winner and a loser; each is determined to be the winner. Eventually, one of them will give up.

It may be Charlotte, who ordinarily takes the verbal victim role. She may throw up her hands and say uncle, accepting the blame and apologizing, not because she feels that she's really to blame but because at that point she will do *any*thing to get the fight over with and go on to bed. Alternatively, she may run from the room crying; or she may start pleading with Jerry to end the argument.

Or it may be *Jerry* who surrenders. Most men have stronger physiological reactions to verbal fights than women do. Their hearts pound harder and their blood pressure surges higher; they start perspiring and feeling nauseated sooner. Women often *look* more upset and are more likely to burst into tears, but most men reach the limit of their physical endurance for verbal combat faster than women do. Some men signal this limit by stamping out of the room and slamming a door behind them. Others bellow their demand for a cease-fire with, "LISten, I just can't TALK about it any LONGer! Will you GIVE it a REST, FOR CRYING OUT LOUD??"

It makes no difference which one gives up first, except in terms of who feels the greatest loss of face: Jerry and Charlotte *both* lose when they handle conflict this way. Each begins the fight with the perception that the other is at fault and that the other "did it on purpose" for negative reasons, such as "to humiliate me." Both end the fight with those perceptions *unchanged*, and with added negative perceptions based on the angry things that were said during the confrontation. And because they realize that there's blame on both sides—though neither one would be willing to admit it—they both end the fight feeling guilty as well as furious.

This is a sure path to a failed relationship.

What to Do about It: Taking Responsibility

Suppose language behavior was not governed by rules; suppose it was not a system but a sort of random "winging it" in which communication success and failure depended on luck and outside circumstances. If that were true, we could say honestly that the whole process was beyond our control. We could then do three convenient things:

- We could use the old "There's nothing I can do!" excuse, with a clear conscience.

- We could claim that we were responsible for the consequences of our language behavior only when we had *deliberately* hurt or misled or confused other people.

- We could throw up our hands and declare that this is just the way the world *is* and that we have no choice but to live with it as best we can.

It is our great good fortune that this is *not* the way the world is, and that we have plenty of choices. Language is a powerful technology in which (unlike the technology of space stations or supercolliders) we are all *experts*. We are all equipped with our internal mental grammars—perfect databases that we can turn to for information whenever we need it.

But with all this privilege comes responsibility. Once we are aware that the language we use has real-world consequences for us and for others, once we know that there are simple and practical actions we can take to affect those consequences for good or for ill, we can no longer sit back and abdicate responsibility. We can no longer sit back and use language without thinking and paying careful attention. We have to take responsibility for it, just as we take responsibility for other behaviors that have a potential for danger, like driving a car.

This process of taking responsibility for our language — not only by eliminating negative elements but also by replacing them with positive ones — involves a number of levels of our grammar. The levels interact and overlap in complicated ways. For purposes of discussion only, we can sort them out as outlined below.

Taking Responsibility at the Level of Sound

* We can eliminate the extra emphatic stresses on words and parts of words that signal hostility.

* We can be careful not to speak so loudly that listening to us is painful, or so softly that listeners must work just to hear what we're saying.

* We can make an effort to speak at a pitch and speed that will be comfortable for those listening to us.

Taking Responsibility at the Level of Vocabulary Choice

* We can eliminate from our speech such openly hostile items as curses and epithets, demeaning or abusive labels, and insults.

* We can avoid choosing words that we know will be unfamiliar to our listeners, or offensive to them.

* We can select words and phrases that will match the sensory modes of people we're interacting with, as a way of actively "speaking their language." And when we can't do that, we can try to avoid using sensory language that will *clash* with others' sensory modes, especially in situations of stress and tension.

* When we can't avoid using words that we know might cause distress or might be misunderstood, we can use them with great care, offering explanations for our choices when that's appropriate.

Taking Responsibility at the Level of Sentence Choice

- We can eliminate from our speech the sentence patterns that are most typical of Blaming and Placating language. And we can use Computing and Leveling patterns when we find ourselves in language interactions that are tense and stressful.

- We can be careful not to use open insults and smart cracks and sarcastic remarks and put-downs.

- We can eliminate the set of English verbal attack patterns from our own speech. And we can systematically discourage their use in others' speech by making sure we don't take their bait and help their attacks succeed.

- We can refuse to provide sentences that feed hostility loops set up by others.

- We can take care not to give other adults direct commands or criticism when we can transmit the same infomation without causing them to lose face — by substituting polite requests and impersonal comments.

All of these strategies are choices that we can freely make for ourselves, whether we are verbal abusers, verbal victims, or involved bystanders. In every case, our goals remain the same: to establish a language environment free of verbal abuse and — when hostility can't be avoided — to deal with it efficiently and effectively. All the strategies work together interdependently to promote this *Gentle Art of Verbal Self-Defense* metastrategy:

✦ As far as possible, never cause anyone to lose face.

One More Technique: Following the Language Traffic Rules

One more level of language behavior, not yet discussed in this book, requires our care and attention. Suppose you are prepared to choose your words, your sentences, and your body language using strategies that will defuse hostility and promote trust and rapport (or, if that's impossible, to promote neutrality). Suppose you are prepared to speak without the characteristics of sound that signal hostility and anger in English, such as extra emphatic stresses or excess volume. That's real progress, and you can be proud of it. However, there's something else you can do to give your communication its maximum positive potential: Follow the *traffic rules* of language.

When drivers cut in front of other cars at intersections, change lanes without warning, refuse to stay *in* their lanes, or drive too slow or too fast, they know they're going to create hostile reactions in other drivers. Most of us don't do those things when we drive, and if we're forced to do them by unusual circumstances, we do our best to let other drivers know what's going on. We know that the goal of traffic on the roads is to get us from place to place, and we know that unless we all follow the same set of rules we're going to waste time (and perhaps risk our health or our lives) in traffic jams and in accidents.

However, when we are involved in language interactions, we may forget that *language is also a kind of traffic*, the goal of which is to move information from person to person. In exactly the same way as with traffic on the road, we need to remember that unless everyone cooperates in language traffic we can't move that information efficiently or satisfactorily. Unless we all follow the rules, we end up wasting our time and taking risks in conversational accidents and communication gridlocks.

There are five basic language traffic violations that make communication difficult, and — if they are our constant habit — tend to become verbal abuse:

1. Interrupting other speakers.

2. Monopolizing conversation, so that other people rarely get a chance to talk.

3. Refusing to talk when it's clearly our *turn* to talk.

4. Failing to support topics introduced by other speakers.

5. Introducing topics that we know will bore or offend other speakers.

So far, so simple — and so obvious. Looking at that list, the tendency is to say, "Oh, that's only good <u>manners</u>!" That's true. But if "only good manners" were the answer, there would *be* no verbal abuse.

All verbal abuse can be avoided if we are careful to use "only good manners" at all times; we aren't. We forget about good manners when we're angry, upset, tired, distressed, or frightened. And we often feel that we shouldn't have to worry about such things when we're in our own homes or workplaces or when we're with people we know well. We say, "They're my <u>family</u>! I don't have to worry about manners with them — they <u>know</u> me!" Or, "Hey, they're my <u>friends</u>! When I'm with them, I can just relax and be myself." Or, "Look — they <u>work</u> for me. If they don't like the way I talk, that's <u>their</u> problem. I don't have time to put on airs with my own employees." Before we make statements like those, natural as they may seem, we need to stop and *think*.

It's true that following the language traffic rules is simple courtesy. So is following traffic rules on the highway. But the reason we stay in our own lane when we drive isn't that we're being polite. We stay in our lane because it's dangerous *not* to, and because we may not get where we're going if we ignore that fact. We need to be aware that the reason for following language traffic rules is also not just to be polite. The real reason is that *if we don't do it, the messages we're trying to send and receive won't arrive, or will arrive damaged.* And the resulting misunderstandings lead straight to the interacting dangers of hostility and loneliness.

Following the language traffic rules requires us to do exactly what we do when we drive a car or truck: We have to pay attention and use our common sense.

When people ignore the rules of the road and an accident happens, it's often impossible to repair the damage. There are injuries and property damage, and it's too late to fix things. In communication accidents, however — if we're paying attention — we can usually do some quick repairs on the spot. Like this:

- "I'm sorry I interrupted you. What were you saying?"

- "I apologize for interrupting — if I don't leave right this minute I'll miss my plane."

- "I'm sorry I changed the subject. Let's go back to what you were telling me."

- "I'm sorry I started talking about autopsies — I wasn't thinking. Let's talk about something more pleasant."

- "I know all this shop talk is boring; forgive me. Let's talk about something more interesting."

- "I haven't been letting anybody else get a word in edgewise; I'm sorry. Your turn!"

- "Wait — I'm doing this all wrong. Let's start over."

This has to be done *honestly* and *sincerely*, however!

Suppose you are someone who always monopolizes the conversation and won't let anyone else talk, but who always — when you're finally ready to stop talking anyway — says, "I haven't been letting anybody else talk; I'm sorry." That's not following the rules, that's a power play; if you do it routinely, it's verbal abuse. Like saying, "I didn't mean anything by it," and "I was only kidding" when people object to language that causes them pain — it's a way of trying to avoid responsibility for your language behavior. It may work now and then, but over time it will fail. People will learn that your apologies are phony, and they will grow more angry every time they hear them.

The same thing is true if you refuse to do your share of the conversational work and people have to struggle for every word they get from you. Or if you consistently interrupt others to finish their sentences. Or if you ignore the subjects others bring up in conversation and switch abruptly to subjects of your own choice. No matter what the violation, *phony* apologies and excuses will not serve as magic incantations that cancel your behavior and make it acceptable to others.

The end result of persistent language traffic violations is always going to be that people will refuse to share the conversational space with the violators, just as they won't willingly share the highways with people who refuse to obey the rules of the road. No matter how potentially important or fascinating the violators' language might otherwise be, it won't be heard — because other people will do everything they can to avoid the violators' company. This means loneliness and isolation, and all their associated penalties.

Fortunately, we can keep this from happening to us. First: We can follow the language traffic rules. Not for abstract philosophical reasons, but because it's dangerous and counterproductive not to. Second: When we genuinely can't follow the rules — and everybody finds themselves in that position once in a while — we can *sincerely* apologize, and we can explain.

Another Look at Scenario Eight

The argument between Charlotte and Jerry Brown in Scenario Eight is a classic example of communication in which *everything* is done wrong. They're not yelling curses at one another, and they're not hitting — but they might as well be. It will be helpful if we take a long look at this massive communication breakdown and do some careful rewriting as we go along.

1. "Jerry," Charlotte said, her voice trembling, "how <u>could</u> you?"

    "How could I <u>what</u>?"

    "<u>YOU</u> know what!"

    "No, I <u>don't</u>, Charlotte! Spell it OUT for me!"

Every line in this sequence is marked by frequent personal language and extra emphatic stresses; it's hostile language, all the way, from both Jerry and Charlotte.

For Charlotte to open a discussion with a chronic verbal abuser like Jerry with "How <u>could</u> you?" guarantees a fight. "How <u>could</u> you?" (and the more explicit "How <u>could</u> you . . ." followed by a description of the behavior) is one of the English verbal attack patterns. It *presupposes that whatever the other person did is absolutely despicable.* It's also a moss-covered dramatic line in the same class as "Be still, my fainting heart!" It's a terrible choice for opening a discussion, and "How could I <u>what</u>?"/YOU know what!" is the almost inevitable follow-up. This is a ritual exchange like "How are you?/I'm fine." The line is appropriate only in the most extreme situations, such as "How <u>could</u> you deLIBerately run over my DOG?" Arguing in front of the boss and his wife doesn't fall into that class. Everything about "How <u>could</u> you?" provides Jerry with an easy path to verbal abuse.

He takes that path — it's his customary strategy for handling conflict in his home — and demands that his offense be "spelled out." But Charlotte doesn't spell it out; instead, she wanders off the subject and hands him yet another golden opportunity, shown in #2.

2. "You know how important that dinner was, to both of us . . . you know how <u>hard</u> I've worked getting ready for — "

    "Oh, THERE we go!" Jerry cut in. "POOR Charlotte! WORK-ING her little FINGERS TO THE bone! Can't you do even ONE simple TASK without making a federal CASE OUT OF IT?"

Charlotte probably did have a legitimate complaint; we know enough about Jerry to assume that early in the evening he said something that was intended to be the opening line in an argument. But we'll never know, because she wanders out of her lane and introduces the topic of the hard work she did getting ready for this important occasion. And Jerry of course leaps at the chance to switch from the subject of his behavior to *hers*.

Charlotte's complaint was presumably, "All evening long, you started one fight after another, in front of our guests!" When she changed lanes before stating it, it disappeared behind *his* complaint, "You can't do even the simplest tasks without exaggerating their difficulty!" That Charlotte then responded to his open abuse with "Jerry, don't try to change the subject," is ironic; she is the one who changed the subject, not Jerry.

3. "Jerry, don't try to change the subject! Please . . . I really want to talk about this."

    "You do? You really want to TALK about the way you dis-GRACED me in front of my BOSS and his WIFE? FINE, Charlotte! Go ahead — TALK!"

"Jerry, that's not FAIR! YOU were the one who STARTED it, every single TIME!"

"Oh, YEAH? How about the time . . ."

The discussion is now completely out of control. And Jerry will be delighted by the opportunity to bring up each of Charlotte's alleged verbal offenses throughout the evening, to be analyzed and fought over. He may have felt powerless and discouraged when the Hendryxes left early, but this altercation with Charlotte allows him to demonstrate to himself and to her that he is *not* powerless. He has the power to get and hold her attention, to tie her up in a long and vicious fight, and to evoke from her the emotional reactions that are supporting evidence of his power.

Charlotte's goal at the beginning of the scenario was to make Jerry understand how disgraceful she believes his behavior was and to make him feel genuinely guilty and remorseful about it. She failed . . . and the chances are 999 to 1 that the fight will end with her saying that *she* is sorry. She makes all the *incorrect linguistic choices,* in terms of achieving her communication goal.

Jerry's goal was to demonstrate his power over Charlotte and to shift the blame for the social disaster from his shoulders to hers if possible. However wrong his language behavior may be in moral terms, he makes all the *right* choices in terms of achieving *his* goals.

Suppose that Charlotte and Jerry were able to communicate in a less disastrous way. The discussion might then have opened like this:

"Jerry," Charlotte said, her voice trembling, "I feel very bad about the way this evening turned out. I think it was a disaster."

"You're right," Jerry answered, slowly. "It was. We did nothing but fight, the whole evening long — Tim and Tina couldn't wait to get out of here."

"Neither one of us <u>wanted</u> things to go so badly," she said, "but it happened anyway. We both had good intentions, we both worked hard to make this dinner a success, and we both failed. We're doing something wrong, Jerry; I just wish I understood what it was so that we could find a way to fix it."

──────────────── ◆ ────────────────

The changes here include the following:

1. Both Charlotte and Jerry are Leveling instead of Blaming.

2. The topic Charlotte introduces to open the conversation is the disastrous *evening*, not Jerry's disastrous *behavior*.

3. Jerry *supports* Charlotte's topic and makes no effort to switch to a new subject of his own choice.

4. No verbal attack patterns are used.

5. Both Charlotte and Jerry use a lot of personal language — but there are no extra stresses on words and parts of words to mark that language as hostile.

6. The personal language is being used to state the simple truth: that both must share the blame for the way their plans went wrong, and that they need to work together to find a solution to their mutual problem.

And what if Jerry's next line is verbal abuse, like this?

"Well, I can tell you what the problem is, Charlotte! It's YOU, and the way you turn EVERYTHING anybody SAYS to you into a FIGHT!"

That could certainly happen. If it does, Charlotte would be wise to resist the temptation to Blame back. Instead, she should lower the level of hostility by opening with a Computing sentence or two, like this:

"Nobody can carry on a fight alone, Jerry. It takes two people, both participating."

and then, with things cooled down, she could switch to Leveling and finish her utterance by saying,

"We need to find some other way to communicate, and I need your help. We've done all the fighting together; whatever we do instead, we'll have to do that together too."

This opening, frankly acknowledging shared blame and proposing that repairing the damage should also be shared, would let these two people discuss their problem without either one losing face or feeling backed against a wall.

For both Jerry and Charlotte, the primary goal needs to be switched from establishing who wins and who loses — as if they were on opposing teams — to how they can work *together* to communicate and establish a language environment free of verbal abuse. The techniques and information presented in this program would put that goal within their reach.

Step 8 Backup

---◆---

Language Traffic Violations Log

This diary page will help you keep track of the language traffic patterns in your life.

DATE: _____

DESCRIPTION OF THE SITUATION:

LANGUAGE TRAFFIC VIOLATION THAT I COMMITTED / THAT I OBSERVED:

WHAT HAPPENED NEXT:

WHAT SHOULD HAVE BEEN DONE INSTEAD:

COMMENTS:

TOTAL NUMBER OF LANGUAGE TRAFFIC VIOLATIONS I'VE COMMITTED SO FAR THIS MONTH: _____

TOTAL NUMBER OF LANGUAGE TRAFFIC VIOLATIONS COMMITTED AGAINST ME SO FAR THIS MONTH: _____

✦ SIGHT BITE ✦
Quotation to Think About and Use

"Language is like a game, we are often told; but if so, it is a game with soft rules; not like chess, played on a board of abstract geometry, but rather like golf, to be played on this actual course or that."

(Vendler 1980, p. 209.)

Conclusion

Nothing has greater power to bring about deep and lasting change than a metaphor; nothing can bring about change more *quickly*.

I can talk to a company for hours, suggesting changes in the way they do business—or I can accomplish the same thing in minutes by explaining that it's time to stop *driving* the business and start *sailing* it.

Every *Star Trek* fan knows that the original creators of that series got nowhere trying to convince the networks to do something so new and so different—until they told them that *Star Trek* was "*Wagon Train* in space."

I spent years feeling resentful when people I visited left their television set on while we were talking. I thought they were rude. I felt that their hospitality was faked, that they didn't really want my company or my conversation. Then one day as I was reading an issue of *Harper's* I came across Camille Paglia's metaphor—*In the modern home, the television set is the flickering fire on the hearth*—and I knew instantly how wrong I had been. I wouldn't have expected my hosts to put out the fire in their fireplace because I was there. I wouldn't have resented the hearthfire's soft noise and light in the background when we talked. Why should I feel any differently about the TV set?

✦ Notice what happened as a result of that metaphor: My hosts were the same people; the TV was the same machine, and no less distracting than before; but my *perception* of the situation was totally changed.

185

Metaphors, and only metaphors, have the power to cause swift and enduring transformation like these. It is ironic and unfortunate that the only instruction most people get about metaphors is in "literature" courses where half a dozen of them—like "My love is a red, red rose"—are pointed out as examples to be tested over. We structure our lives around metaphors, and they constantly filter our perceptions of reality; we need to learn much more about them and take them far more seriously.

The Unifying Metaphor in Verbal Abuse

Both verbal abusers and verbal victims in our culture typically filter *their* perceptions of their world through this single ugly and brutal metaphor:

◆ LIFE IS A TORTURE CHAMBER.

Life is a torture chamber, where the verbal abuser is the Torturer, getting wicked sadistic pleasure from the pain of the victim; where the verbal victim is the Torture Victim, defenseless and doomed to suffer; and where, if the victim finds any pleasure in life at all, it is the twisted pleasure of the masochist, who seeks out pain. In the reality created by this metaphor, words are whips and knives and fists; conversations are interrogations and ordeals; relationships are bondage for which the only solution is escape; homes and workplaces are prisons; and hope is folly. It is no wonder people get sick, in such an environment!

What to Do about It

If You're a Verbal Abuser

Set aside for once and for all the idea that you are *wicked*. It's not true. It's a myth, invented by the culture of violence and fed by the people who believe in it. You're not wicked. You're not cruel. You don't take pleasure in others' pain. When you try to excuse your language behavior with "I didn't *mean* to hurt anybody!" you are telling the truth. Don't let anyone tell you differently.

Imagine a person who grew up believing that the only way to get food was to steal it. When such a person—driven by hunger—stole a meal, you wouldn't call that wickedness. You yourself, if you were hungry enough and had no other options, would steal food, even if you are someone who ordinarily wouldn't even steal a paper clip—and you wouldn't call that wickedness.

The problem is that in our society we know a tremendous amount about physical hunger, but we know far too little about the equally powerful and compelling emotional hunger of the *spirit*. When I talk to chronic verbal abusers who are having a hard time giving up the habit of verbal violence, they usually spend quite a while claiming that what they do is really harmless and that only wimps and weaklings worry about verbal violence. And then, when they've begun trusting me, they say things like this:

"I'm sorry—I just really get a <u>kick</u> out of kidding <u>around</u> with people!"

"I love to <u>argue</u>, <u>that's</u> all! It's a heck of a lot of <u>fun</u>!"

"Hey, I <u>enjoy</u> batting stuff back and forth, getting people's goat, kind of finding out how much excitement I can generate! It's a <u>high</u>, you <u>know</u>?"

✦ That is: "Verbal abuse feeds my spirit."

The human body needs physical food; human beings will work to find and guard and maintain a food supply. In desperate circumstances they will do things to obtain food that they wouldn't ordinarily consider doing. In just the same way, they need *emotional* food, and one of the primary sources of such nourishment is the attention of other human beings—attention that can be reliably obtained only by interacting with others. The need for that human attention is fierce; it drives us just as physical hunger does. Verbal abusers are in the same situation as people who think they can get food only by stealing it: They take attention by force, not because they are sadistic but because they don't know how to get others to give it to them voluntarily.

If you are a verbal abuser, you need an opportunity to experience the pleasure that comes from receiving attention that is willingly and freely given. Good conversation provides the same "high" — the same exchange of attention, the same intense mutual participation, the same pleasure in shared emotions — that you now find in what is called "a good fight." After you've had that experience, you will be more than willing to give up the satisfaction that you can get only by causing a listener pain.

The verbal violence "high" has grave penalties attached to it. There's your victims' resentment, the grudges they hold against you, and the attempts they make to even the score. There's the inevitable loneliness that comes from being someone whose company other people will avoid if they possibly can. There's the guilt you feel when you know you've caused someone pain, however much you may try to deny its reality. There's the serious hazard to your own health and the health of your victims. And if you have children, there's your knowledge that you are training them to grow up and be verbal abusers, too, who will then face all the same penalties. *Good* communication, free of verbal abuse, carries none of these negatives with it.

If You're a Verbal Victim

One thing that verbal abusers and verbal victims have in common is the "helpless" label. But there's a difference. For abusers the claim is that they're helpless to change because they're wicked. For verbal victims (with the exception of those who are accused of being masochists), the claim is that they are helpless to change not because they are wicked but because they're weak.

If you are a verbal victim, you need to set aside the idea that you are weak. You're not weak. It takes a great deal of *strength* to endure life in an environment of verbal violence. It takes courage to get up every day and face your tormentor(s) again. It takes courage and strength to keep your life going when you know what you're facing and you don't feel that you have any way out. That's not weakness — but it is a great *waste* of your strength.

There are two typical reasons for the verbal victim's behavior. Sometimes it's a simple lack of information. Like Charlotte Brown in the scenarios, the verbal victim may be unaware that any other way to handle verbal conflict exists.

Sometimes the problem is that verbal victims recognize the need for the role they are playing, and feel an obligation to fill it *for the sake of the abuser, for the sake of their relationship with the abuser, or both.* This isn't necessarily an idea they're consciously aware of; often they will reject it vigorously if it's suggested to them. But at some level of consciousness they are convinced that they *must* fill the victim role.

They feel that the stability of the relationship — as husband and wife, or parent and child, or boss and employee, or friend and friend — depends on their continuing to serve as victim. They are convinced that the relationship would collapse if they no longer participated in the verbal violence, or they are convinced that the well-being of the abuser depends critically on their doing so. When the relationship matters enough to them, they're willing to tolerate their pain in order to preserve it; when their love for the abuser is great enough, they're willing to tolerate their pain for the abuser's sake. (It is this situation that often is labeled "codependency.") This, too, is a lack of information, but the problem is more complicated.

You have to begin by giving up the idea that you are weak and helpless. You have to recognize your own strength. You have to understand that a life of chronic hostility is *dangerous* for the verbal abuser. And you need to become aware that there is a *better* way to build a stable relationship than by doing a life sentence at hard verbal labor. You can take the same strength that you've been using all along — to stand up under verbal abuse and to carry on your life in spite of the burden — and use it differently. You can put that strength and energy into creating a relationship of mutual respect, free of verbal violence, with tremendous advantages for both you and the former verbal abuser(s). And if you have children, this comes with the added bonus of knowing that you're not training *them* to be verbal victims and abusers too.

If You're an Involved Bystander

You need to know just one thing: that you serve *no* useful purpose, for yourself or for anyone else, when you participate in other people's verbal violence. If you sit silently, taking no direct part, the very fact that you don't leave implies that you're willing to accept what's going on. If you try to openly intercede for the victim, you reinforce the idea that he or she is helpless and needs to be rescued by others. Only rarely will there be any way that you can help by staying.

What you *can* do is provide the verbal abuser and victim with resources for solving the problem on their own. Get them to read this book, for example. And when you have the opportunity, model for them the communication strategies for handling conflict that you've learned from working through this program.

———————————— ◆ ————————————

The ancient proverb says: *A soft answer turneth away wrath.* The problem for our society has been the mistaken idea that "soft answers" could only be weak and submissive answers that require the sacrifice of dignity and principle. In this eight-step program we have discovered that we have available to us a vast array of soft answers — gentle answers — that have none of those negative characteristics and that represent language we can use with confidence and honor. We have also learned that we are already equipped with everything we need to begin using our language positively rather than negatively.

When we eliminate verbal abuse from our lives, we get rid of nothing that is worth keeping. We reduce tension and stress, and we increase opportunities for health and happiness, not only for ourselves but for everyone we interact with. When we eliminate verbal violence, we have also begun to eliminate physical violence.

Cleaning up the language environment by getting rid of the toxic language and replacing it with wholesome language is not just another way to improve our personal image. *It is literally a way to save this Earth.*

If you are involved in chronic verbal violence, whether as abuser or victim or involved bystander, it's time to abandon that destructive and terrifying metaphor. It's time to come out of the Torture Chamber and close its door behind you. It has no reality except the reality *you* give it in your own mind and through your own participation in verbal abuse. You have the power not just to survive it, but to shut it down forever. The good news is: *You don't have to live in there any longer.*

This book is the key to the door.

✦ SIGHT BITES ✦
Quotations to Think About and Use

"Metaphor is the matrix for understanding. It is the language of personal transformation."

(Brown 1991, p. xi.)

"My miracle is not that you can't knock me down, my miracle is that I know how to get up. And I can teach *you* how to get up."

(Gaskin n.d., p. 83.)

"Parents need to ask whether they're teaching their children tolerance, and to be nonviolent. We're going to have to come to grips with this because we keep blaming someone else for the . . . glorification of violence in our society."

(M. Edelman, quoted in Granat 1992, p. 43.)

"The family is a self-correcting system that governs itself through rules established over a period of time by trial and error."

(Burbatti and Formenti 1988, p. 13.)

Bibliography

Articles

Addington, D. W. "The Relationship of Selected Vocal Characteristics to Personality Perception." *Speech Monographs* 35 (1968): 492–503.

A.F.G. "Notes: Judges' Nonverbal Behavior in Jury Trials: A Threat to Judicial Impartiality." *Virginia Law Review* 61 (1975): 1266–98.

Albert, M. "Universal Grammar." *Z*, December 1988, pp. 99–104.

Beattie, G. W. "Interruption in Conversational Interaction, and Its Relation to the Sex and Status of the Interactants." *Linguistics* 19 (1981): 15–35.

_____. "The Regulation of Speaker-Turns in Face-to-Face Conversation: Some Implications for Conversation in Sound-Only Communication Channels." *Semiotica* 34 (1981): 55–70.

Beckman, H. B., and R. M. Frankel. "The Effect of Physician Behavior on the Collection of Data." *Annals of Internal Medicine,* November 1984, pp. 692–6.

Bell, C. "Family Violence." *JAMA,* 19 September 1986, pp. 1501–2.

Blakeslee, S. "Cynicism and Mistrust Tied to Early Death." *New York Times,* 17 January 1989.

Blanck, P. D. "The Appearance of Justice: Judges' Verbal and Nonverbal Behavior in Criminal Jury Trials." *Stanford Law Review,* November 1985, pp. 89–163.

_____. "Off the Record: Nonverbal Communication in the Courtroom." *Stanford Lawyer,* Spring 1987, pp. 18–23, 39.

_____. "What Empirical Research Tells Us: Studying Judges' and Juries' Behavior." *American University Law Review* 40 (1991): 775–804.

Bolinger, D. "Contrastive Accent and Contrastive Stress." *Language* 37 (1961): 83–96.

Cassileth, B. R., et al. "Psychosocial Correlates of Survival in Advanced

Malignant Disease." *New England Journal of Medicine,* 13 June 1985, pp. 1551–5.

Check, W. E. "Homicide, Suicide, Other Violence Gain Increasing Medical Attention." *JAMA,* 9 August 1985, pp. 721–30.

Cosmides, L. "Invariance in the Acoustic Expression of Emotion during Speech." *Journal of Experimental Psychology,* December 1983, pp. 864–81.

Dimsdale, J. E. "A Perspective on Type A Behavior and Coronary Disease." *New England Journal of Medicine,* 14 January 1988, pp. 110–12.

Douglas, C. "The Beat Goes On." *Psychology Today,* November 1987, pp. 38–42.

Easterbrook, G. "The Revolution in Modern Medicine." *Newsweek,* 16 January 1987, pp. 40–74.

Easton, N. J. "It's Cool to Be Cruel: Forget the Niceties, America Is on a Mean Streak." *Dallas Morning News,* 4 July 1993.

Edelsky, C. "Who's Got the Floor?" *Language in Society* 10 (1981), 383–421.

Ehrenreich, B. "The Politics of Talking in Couples." *MS,* May 1981, pp. 46, 48.

Epstein, S. E., et al. "Myocardial Ischemia — Silent or Symptomatic." *New England Journal of Medicine,* 21 April 1988, pp. 1038–43.

Ervin-Tripp, S., et al. "Language and Power in the Family." In C. Kramarae et al., eds., *Language and Power* (Beverly Hills, CA: Sage, 1984), pp. 116–35.

Feiner, B. (Interview with Candace West.) "Communication Breakdowns: Are Your Patients Turned Off?" *Options,* August 1986, pp. 33–6.

Fellman, B. "A Conversation with Ira Progoff." *Medical Self-Care,* July-August 1978, pp. 11–12.

_____. "Talk: The Not-So-Silent Killer." *Science* 85, December 1985, pp. 70–1.

Fincher, J. "Inside an Intensive Journal Workshop." *Medical Self-Care,* July-August 1978, pp. 6–10.

Finkbeiner, A. "The Puzzle of Child Abuse." *Science Illustrated,* June-July 1987, pp. 14–19.

Fox, B. H. "Depression Symptoms and Cancer." *JAMA,* 1 September 1989, p. 1231.

Friedman, M. "Type A Behavior and Mortality from Coronary Heart Disease." *New England Journal of Medicine,* 14 July 1988, p. 114. (See also other letters under same title, through p. 117.)

Gold, P. W., et al. "Clinical and Biochemical Manifestations of Depression: Relation to Neurobiology of Stress." (In two parts.) *New England Journal of Medicine,* Part 1: 11 August 1988, pp. 348–51; Part 2: 18 August 1988, pp. 413–20.

Goldberg, J. "Anatomy of a Scientific Discovery." *Science Illustrated,* January-February 1989, pp. 5–12.

Goleman, D. "Studies Point to Power of Nonverbal Signals." *New York Times,* 8 April 1986.

_____. "Research Affirms Power of Positive Thinking." *New York Times,* 3 February 1987.

_____. "The Mind Over the Body." *New York Times Magazine,* 27 September 1987, pp. 36–39, 59–60.

_____. "Researchers Find That Optimism Helps the Body's Defense System." *New York Times,* 20 April 1989.

_____. "Researchers Trace Empathy's Roots to Infancy." *New York Times,* 28 April 1989.

_____. "A Feel-Good Theory: A Smile Affects Mood." *New York Times,* 18 July 1989.

_____. "Sensing Silent Cues Emerges As Key Skill." *New York Times,* 10 October 1989.

Gorman, C. "Can't Afford to Get Sick." *Time,* 21 August 1989, p. 43.

Granat, D. "Mother Knows Best." *Washingtonian,* November 1992, pp. 41–5.

Gray, F., et al. "Little Brother Is Changing You." *Psychology Today,* March 1974, pp. 42–6.

Greydanus, D. E. "Risk-Taking Behaviors in Adolescence." *Journal of the American Medical Association,* 16 October 1987, p. 2110.

Groden, J. "Children with Asthma Breathing Easier." *Mind-Body-Health Digest* 3:1 (1988): 3–4.

Growald, E. R., and A. Luks. "The Immunity of Samaritans: Beyond Self." *American Health,* March 1988, pp. 51–3.

Haden, R. "A Comparative Exploration of the Expression of Anger in Fourteen Languages, and Some Implications." *Arktesol Post,* Summer-Fall 1987, pp. 7–10.

Hall, E. "Giving Away Psychology in the 80's: George Miller Interviewed by Elizabeth Hall." *Psychology Today,* January 1980, pp. 38–50, 97–8.

Hall, S. S. "A Molecular Code Links Emotions, Mind and Health." *Smithsonian,* June 1989, pp. 62–71.

Harris, T. G. "Heart and Soul." *Psychology Today,* January-February 1989, pp. 50–2.

Harvey, J. B. "The Abilene Paradox: The Management of Agreement." *Organizational Dynamics,* Summer 1974, pp. 1–18.

Higgins, L. C. "Hostility Theory Rekindles Debate over Type A Behavior." *Medical World News,* February 27, 1989, p. 21.

Hollien, M. "Vocal Indicators of Psychological Stress." *Annals of the New York Academy of Science* 347 (1980): 47–72.

House, J. S., et al. "Social Relationships and Health." *Science,* 29 July 1988, pp. 540–4.

Jones, E. E. "Interpreting Interpersonal Behavior: The Effects of Expectancies." *Science,* 3 October 1986, pp. 41–6.

Kamiya, G. "The Cancer Personality." *Hippocrates,* November-December 1989, pp. 92–3.

Kobasa, S. O. "Test for Hardiness: How Much Stress Can You Survive? *American Health,* September 1984, p. 64.

Kochakian, M. J. "Those Youngsters Out of Synch." *Gannett Suburban Newspapers,* 18 May 1992.

Kohn, A. "Beyond Selfishness." *Psychology Today,* October 1988, pp. 34–8.

Krier, B. A. "Conversation Interruptus: Critical Social Skill or Just Plain Rudeness?" *Los Angeles Times,* 14 December 1986.

Lynch, J. J. "Interpersonal Aspects of Blood Pressure Control." *Journal of Nervous and Mental Diseases* 170 (1982): 143–53.

———. "Listen and Live." *American Health,* April 1985, pp. 39–43.

McConnell-Ginet, S. "Intonation in a Man's World." In B. Thorne et al., eds., *Language, Gender, and Society* (Rowley, MA: Newbury House, 1983), pp. 69–88.

Miller, G. "Giving Away Psychology in the 80's." *Psychology Today,* January 1980, pp. 38–50 and 97–98.

Miller, S. M. "Why Having Control Reduces Stress: If I Can Stop the Roller Coaster I Don't Have to Get Off." In J. Garber and M. E. P. Seligman, eds., *Human Helplessness: Theory and Applications* (New York: Academic Press, 1980).

Milstead, J. "Verbal Battering." *BBW,* August 1985, pp. 34–5, 61, 68.

Miron, M. S., and T. A. Pasquale. "Psycholinguistic Analysis of Coercive Communication." *Journal of Psycholinguistic Research* 7 (1985): 95–120.

Olsen, E., et al. "Beyond Positive Thinking." *Success,* December 1988, pp. 31–38.

Oppenheim, G. "How to Defuse a Hostile Patient." *Medical Economics,* 5 September 1988, pp. 125–34.

Parlee, M. B. "Conversational Politics," *Psychology Today,* May 1979, pp. 45–86.

Phillips, P. "Domestic Violence on the Increase." *Cortlandt Forum,* November 1992, pp. 48DD–48EE.

Pines, M. "Psychological Hardiness: The Role of Challenge in Health." *Psychology Today,* December 1980, pp. 34–45.

Rauch, J. "The Humanitarian Threat to Free Inquiry." *Reason,* April 1993, pp. 21–27.

Rozanski, A., et al. "Mental Stress and the Induction of Silent Myocardial Ischemia in Patients with Coronary Artery Disease." *New England Journal of Medicine,* 21 April 1986, pp. 1005–12.

Sacks, H., et al. "A Simplest Systematics for the Organization of Turn-Taking for Conversation." *Language* 50 (1974), pp. 696–735.

Scherwitz, L., et al. "Self-Involvement and the Risk Factors for Coronary Heart Disease." *Advances,* Winter 1985, pp. 6–18.

Seligman, J., et al. "Emotional Child Abuse: Discipline's Fine Line." *Newsweek,* 3 October 1988, pp. 48–50.

_____. "The Wounds of Words: When Verbal Abuse Is as Scary as Physical Abuse." *Newsweek,* 12 October 1992, pp. 90–2.

Shea, M. J. "Mental Stress and the Heart." *CVR&R,* April 1988, pp. 51–8.

Shuy, R. W. "The Medical Interview: Problems in Communication." *Primary Care,* September 1976, pp. 365–86.

Tavris, C. "Anger Defused." *Psychology Today,* November 1982, pp. 25–35.

Troemel-Ploetz, S. "Review Essay: Selling the Apolitical." (Review of Tannen 1990.) *Discourse & Society,* October 1991, pp. 489–502.

Ueland, B. "Tell Me More: On the Fine Art of Listening." *Utne Reader,* November-December 1992, pp. 104–9.

Vendler, Z. Review of P. Cole, *Syntax and Semantics,* vol. 9. *Language,* March 1980, pp. 209–14.

Weiner, E. J. "A Knowledge Representation Approach to Understanding Metaphors." *Computational Linguistics* 10 (1984): 1–14.

West, C., and A. Garcia. "Conversational Shift Work: A Study of Topical Transitions Between Women and Men." *Social Problems* 35 (1988): 551–75.

Williams, R. "Curing Type A: The Trusting Heart." *Psychology Today,* January-February 1989, pp. 36–42.

_____. "The Trusting Heart." *New Age Journal,* May-June 1989, pp. 26–30, 101.

Wright, H. N. "Toxic Talk." *Christian Parenting Today,* July-August 1991, pp. 24–30.

Zajonc, R. B. "Emotion and Facial Efference: A Theory Reclaimed." *Science,* 5 April 1985, pp. 15–20.

Zal, H. M. "The Psychiatric Aspects of Myocardial Infarction." *Cardiovascular Reviews & Reports,* February 1987, pp. 33–7.

Zimmerman, J. "Does Emotional State Affect Disease?" *MD,* April 1986, pp. 30, 41–3.

Zonderman, A. B., et al. "Depression as a Risk for Cancer Morbidity and Mortality in a Nationally Representative Sample." *JAMA,* 1 September 1989, pp. 1191–5.

Items with No Byline

"The Art of Negotiation." *Royal Bank Letter,* July-August 1986, pp. 1–4.

"Chronic Headache: Predict the Outcome at the First Visit." *Modern Medicine,* December 1986, pp. 96, 101.

"Communication Breakdowns." *Options,* August 1986, pp. 33–7. (Interview with Candace West.)

"Consensus Conference: Differential Diagnosis of Dementing Diseases." *JAMA,* 18 December 1987, pp. 3411–6.

"Group Therapy Support Increases Cancer Survival." *Brain/Mind Bulletin,* August 1989, p. 1.

"How Hostile Thinking Makes You Heart-Sick." *Your Personal Best,* April 1989.

"Image and Likeness." (Interview with Bishop Kallistos Ware.) *Parabola,* Spring 1985, pp. 62–71.

Review of Ira Progoff, *At a Journal Workshop* (New York: Dialogue House Library 1975). *Medical Self-Care,* July-August 1978, pp. 4–5.

"Swiftness of Spouse's Death Affects Mate's Mortality Risk." *Medical World News,* 11 September 1989, p. 27.

Books

Ader, R., ed. *Psychoneuroimmunology.* New York: Academic Press, 1981.

Antonovsky, A. *Health, Stress, and Coping.* San Francisco: Jossey-Bass, 1979.

Argyle, M. *Bodily Communication.* London: Methuen, 1975.

Barsy, A. J. *Worried Sick: Our Troubled Quest for Wellness.* Boston: Little, Brown, 1988.

Beattie, G. *Talk: An Analysis of Speech and Non-Verbal Behaviour in Conversation.* Milton Keynes, England: Open University Press, 1983.

Beck, A., and A. Katcher. *Between Pets and People: The Importance of Animal Companionship.* New York: Putnam, 1983.

Benson, H. *The Mind/Body Effect.* New York: Simon & Schuster, 1979.

Benson, H., and W. Proctor. *Beyond the Relaxation Response.* New York: Times Books, 1984.

Blumenthal, M. D., et al. *More about Justifying Violence: Methodological Studies of Attitudes and Behavior.* Ann Arbor: University of Michigan, 1975.

Bolinger, D. *Intonation.* Harmondsworth: Penguin Books, 1972.

Bolton, R. *People Skills: How to Assert Yourself, Listen to Others and Resolve Conflicts.* Englewood Cliffs, NJ: Prentice-Hall, 1979.

Borysenko, J. (with L. Rothstein). *Minding the Body, Mending the Mind.* Reading, MA: Addison-Wesley, 1987.

Brown, P. *The Hypnotic Brain: Hypnotherapy and Social Communication.* New Haven, CT: Yale University Press, 1991.

Burbatti, G. L., and L. Formenti. *The Milan Approach to Family Therapy.* Northvale, NJ: Jason Aronson, 1988.

Cassell, E. J. *Talking with Patients,* Vol. 1: *Theory of Doctor-Patient Communication;* Vol. 2: *Clinical Technique.* Cambridge, MA: MIT Press, 1985.

Charlesworth, E. A., and R. G. Nathan. *Stress Management: A Comprehensive Guide to Wellness.* New York: Ballantine, 1982.

Chesney, M., and R. H. Rosenman, eds. *Anger and Hostility in Cardiovascular and Behavioral Disorders.* Washington, DC: Hemisphere Corporation, 1985.

Clark, V. P., et al., eds. *Language: Introductory Readings.* 3rd ed. New York: St. Martin's Press, 1981.

Craig, R. T., and K. Tracy. *Conversational Coherence: Form, Structure, and Strategy.* Beverly Hills, CA: Sage, 1983.

Elgin, S. H. *What Is Linguistics?* 2nd ed. Englewood Cliffs, NJ: Prentice-Hall, 1979.

_____. *More on the Gentle Art of Verbal Self-Defense.* New York: Prentice-Hall, 1983.

_____. *The Gentle Art of Verbal Self-Defense.* New York: Barnes & Noble, 1985. [Originally published by Prentice-Hall, 1980.]

_____. *Language in Emergency Medicine: A Verbal Self-Defense/Syntonics Handbook.* Huntsville, AR: Ozark Center for Language Studies, 1987a.

_____. *The Last Word on the Gentle Art of Verbal Self-Defense.* Englewood Cliffs, NJ: Prentice-Hall, 1987b.

_____. *Success with the Gentle Art of Verbal Self-Defense.* Englewood Cliffs, NJ: Prentice-Hall, 1989.

_____. *Mastering the Gentle Art of Verbal Self-Defense.* Englewood Cliffs, NJ: Prentice-Hall, 1989. [Audio program.]

_____. *Manual for Gentle Art Syntonics Trainers,* Vol. 1: *Level One.* Huntsville, AR: Ozark Center for Language Studies, 1990.

_____. *Staying Well with the Gentle Art of Verbal Self-Defense.* Englewood Cliffs, NJ: Prentice-Hall, 1991.

_____. *The Gentle Art of Written Self-Defense.* Englewood Cliffs, NJ: Prentice-Hall, 1993.

Elgin, S. H., and R. Haden, M.A. *Raising Civilized Kids in a Savage World.* Huntsville, AR: Ozark Center for Language Studies, 1989.

Ekman, P., et al. *Emotion in the Human Face.* New York: Pergamon, 1972.

Fisher, S. *In the Patient's Best Interest: Women and the Politics of Medical Decisions.* New Brunswick, NJ: Rutgers University Press, 1986.

Fisher, S., and A. D. Todd. *The Social Organization of Doctor-Patient Communication.* Washington, DC: Center for Applied Linguistics, 1983.

Frank, J. *Persuasion and Healing.* Baltimore, MD: Johns Hopkins, 1973.

Friedman, M., and R. H. Rosenman. *Type A Behavior and Your Heart.* New York: Knopf, 1974.

Friedman, M., and D. Ulmer. *Treating Type A Behavior and Your Heart.* New York: Knopf, 1984.

Gaskin, S. *Monday Night Class.* San Francisco: Book Publishing Company, n.d.

Gordon, T. *Leader Effectiveness Training: L.E.T.* New York: Wyden Books, 1977.

Hall, E. T. *The Silent Language.* New York: Doubleday Anchor, 1959.

_____. *Beyond Culture.* New York: Doubleday Anchor, 1977.

Justice, B. *Who Gets Sick?: Thinking and Health.* Houston: Peak Press, 1987.

Katz, J. *The Silent World of Doctor and Patient.* New York: Macmillan, Free Press, 1984.

Key, M. R. *Male/Female Language.* Metuchen, NJ: Scarecrow Press, 1975.

_____, ed. *The Relationship of Verbal and Nonverbal Communication.* The Hague: Mouton, 1980.

Kramarae, C., ed. *The Voices and Words of Women and Men.* Oxford: Pergamon Press, 1980.

Lakoff, G., and M. Johnson. *Metaphors We Live By.* Chicago: University of Chicago Press, 1980.

Lakoff, R. *Talking Power: The Politics of Language in Our Lives.* New York: Basic Books, 1990.

Lazarus, R. S., and S. Folkman. *Stress, Appraisal, and Coping.* New York: Springer, 1984.

Leech, G. *Principles of Pragmatics.* London: Longman, 1983.

Levy, S. M. *Behavior and Cancer.* San Francisco: Jossey-Bass, 1985.

Locke, S., et al., eds. *Foundations of Psychoneuroimmunology.* New York: Aldine, 1985.

Locke, S., and D. Colligan. *The Healer Within: The New Medicine of Mind and Body.* New York: New American Library, Mentor, 1987.

Lynch, J. J. *The Broken Heart: The Medical Consequences of Loneliness.* New York: Basic Books, 1977.

_____. *The Language of the Heart: The Body's Response to Human Dialogue.* New York: Basic Books, 1985.

O'Barr, W. M. *Linguistic Evidence: Language, Power, and Strategy in the Courtroom.* New York: Academic Press, 1982.

Ornstein, R., and D. Sobel. *The Healing Brain: Breakthrough Discoveries about How the Brain Keeps Us Healthy.* New York: Simon & Schuster, 1987.

Ornstein, R., and C. Swencious, eds. *The Healing Brain: A Scientific Reader.* New York: Guilford Press, 1990.

Peale, N. V. *The Power of Positive Thinking.* Englewood Cliffs, NJ: Prentice-Hall, 1961.

Postman, N. *Crazy Talk, Stupid Talk: How We Defeat Ourselves by the Way We Talk—And What to Do about It.* New York: Dell, 1961.

Progoff, I. *At a Journal Workshop.* New York: Dialogue House, 1975.

Rainer, T. *The New Diary.* Los Angeles: Jeremy P. Tarcher, 1978.

Rendema, J. *Discourse Studies: An Introductory Textbook.* Philadelphia: John Benjamins, 1993.

Rothwell, J. D. *Telling It Like It Isn't.* Englewood Cliffs, NJ: Prentice-Hall, 1982.

Satir, V. *Conjoint Family Therapy.* Palo Alto, CA: Science & Behavior Books, 1964.

_____. *Peoplemaking.* Palo Alto, CA: Science & Behavior Books, 1972.

Sattel, J. W. *Men, Inexpressivensss, and Power.* Rowley, MA: Newbury House, 1983.

Tannen, D. *That's Not What I Meant! How Conversational Style Makes or Breaks Relationships.* New York: William Morrow, 1986.

_____. *You Just Don't Understand: Women and Men in Conversation.* New York: William Morrow, 1990.

Thorne, B., and N. Henley, eds. *Language and Sex, Difference and Dominance.* Rowley, MA: Newbury House, 1975.

Thorne, B., et al., eds. *Language, Gender and Society.* Rowley, MA: Newbury House, 1983.

Todd, A. D. *Intimate Adversaries: Cultural Conflict Between Doctors and Women Patients.* Philadelphia: University of Pennsylvania Press, 1989.

Van Dijk, T. A., ed. *Handbook of Discourse Analysis.* London: Academic Press, 1985.

Watts, A. *Beyond Theology: The Art of Godmanship.* Cleveland, OH: World Publishing Co., 1967.

Watzlawick, P., et al. *Pragmatics of Human Communication: A Study of Interactional Patterns, Pathologies, and Paradoxes.* New York: Norton, 1967.

West, C. *Routine Complications: Troubles with Talk Between Doctors and Patients.* Bloomington: Indiana University Press, 1984.

Young-Eisendrath, P., Ph.D. *You're Not What I Expected: Learning to Love the Opposite Sex.* New York: William Morrow, 1993.

Index to Backup Material

Index

205